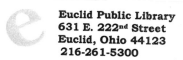

TRANNY

TRANNY

CONFESSIONS OF PUNK ROCK'S
MOST INFAMOUS ANARCHIST SELLOUT

LAURA JANE GRACE
with DAN OZZI

NEW YORK • BOSTON

Copyright © 2016 by Total Treble, LLC

Cover design and interior design by Christopher Norris/Steak Mtn
Cover copyright © 2016 by Hachette Book Group, Inc.

Hachette Books
Hachette Book Group
1290 Avenue of the Americas
New York, NY 10104
hachettebookgroup.com
twitter.com/hachettebooks

First edition: November 2016

Photos courtesy of the author, except for the following: (page 4, top) Joe Leonard, (page 5, bottom) Bryan Wynacht, (page 6, top) Bryan Wynacht, (page 7, top) Wes Orshowski, (page 7, bottom) Ryan Russell, (page 8, top) Jason Thrasher, (page 8, middle) Ryan Russell, (page 8, bottom) Ryan Russell

Hachette Books is a division of Hachette Book Group, Inc.
The Hachette Books name and logo are trademarks of Hachette Book Group, Inc.

The publisher is not responsible for websites (or their content) that are not owned by the publisher.

The Hachette Speakers Bureau provides a wide range of authors for speaking events. To find out more, go to www.hachettespeakersbureau.com or call (866) 376-6591.

Library of Congress Cataloging-in-Publication Data

Names: Grace, Laura Jane, 1980- author. | Ozzi, Dan author.
Title: Tranny : confessions of punk rock's most infamous anarchist sellout / Laura Jane Grace with Dan Ozzi.
Description: First edition. | New York : Hachette Books, 2016.
Identifiers: LCCN 2016028515| ISBN 9780316387958 (hardcover) | ISBN 9780316264389 (ebook) | ISBN 9781478943372 (audio cd) | ISBN 9781478940180 (audio download)
Subjects: LCSH: Grace, Laura Jane, 1980– | Punk rock musicians—United States—Biography. | Transgender musicians—United States—Biography. | Against Me! (Musical group)
Classification: LCC ML420.G7835 A3 2016 | DDC 782.42166092 [B]—dc23
LC record available at https://lccn.loc.gov/2016028515

Printed in the United States of America

LSC-C

10 9 8 7 6 5 4 3

For Evelyn

CONTENTS

TRANNY

I. WALKING IS STILL HONEST

It was 1985 and I was five years old, still young enough to think the lyrics to Madonna's song "Material Girl" were "I am a Cheerio girl." I stood in the glow of the television in my family's living room, watching her movements in stunned, silent awe.

My parents liked music, but weren't fanatical about it. My father enjoyed country and in particular Willie Nelson, while my mother's favorite was Diana Ross and the Supremes. But something about this pop star spoke to me. Watching Madonna get into the groove, I was completely mesmerized.

Her dirty blond hair was moussed and frizzed to perfection. Her neon and black clothes were ripped and torn to accentuate her curves. Her chunky bracelets and necklaces sparkled and jangled against her arms and neck as she moved to the beat. I reached out my hand and touched her on the screen. *That's me,* I thought, clear as day. I wanted to do that. I wanted to *be* that.

This sense of wonderment was cut short by confusion. Suddenly I realized that I would never be her, that I could never be her. Madonna was a girl; a confident symbol of femininity, singing and dancing onstage in a short skirt and high heels. I was just a small boy, living in a ranch house on an Army base in Fort Hood, Texas.

My father's name was Thomas. My uncle's name was Thomas. My cousin's name was Thomas. And I was born Thomas James Gabel, the son of a soldier, a West Point graduate who never went to war. That was the name written on my birth certificate, but I never felt that it suited me.

I was born on November 8, 1980, in Chattahoochee County, Georgia, though I would never claim to be from the South. I was from Tobyhanna, Pennsylvania, and Cincinnati, Ohio, and Lago Patria, Italy. My family packed up our lives every few years and moved to a new station, wherever my father was assigned. Being an Army brat made me a traveling soul from birth, introducing me to new people and new friends, teaching me about different cultures around the world and how to adapt to new ways of life.

Even as a toddler, I was a naturally destructive force. When my mother took me grocery shopping, from my seat in the cart, I kept grabbing items off the shelves and tossing them on the ground. "Tom!" she'd scold. "Tom...Tom!" The stern older man working the register once watched my mother's plight and muttered, "Tom Tom the Atom Bomb." After that, the name stuck.

My parents weren't deeply religious people, but would occasionally drag me and my brother, Mark, who was six years my junior, to church. They were both raised Catholic, but our church denomination didn't seem to matter to them—Presbyterian, Methodist, whatever was most socially convenient with other

Army officers. As for me, I was fairly indifferent about religion, as long as I didn't end up burning in hell.

After church on Sundays, I would build forts with blankets and sheets, covering my bedroom from corner to corner. Underneath those bedding canopies I created a world of my own, my first experiences with privacy from my parents. To save space on storage, my mother kept her nylons in my bottom dresser drawer. I found them, and natural curiosity led me to try them on. I wondered what was so special about these shriveled brown socks that only my mom got to wear.

In the dark secrecy of my forts, I lay on my back, stretched my legs up toward the sky, and slowly rolled the nylons down over my legs. I was almost hypnotized by the sensation of nylon on skin.

This must be what it feels like to be a woman, I thought to myself.

My father would walk by and see the sheets and blanket tent tops I had constructed over the furniture.

"Tommy, what the hell are you doing in there?" he'd bark.

"Nothing!" I'd call back, and I would roll the nylons off my legs and hide them as quick as I could. No one ever had to tell me that what I was doing in my fort was indecent behavior. I could just feel that it was wrong, as if I was born with the shame. I had already been caught playing Barbies with a neighbor girl. My father's reaction was a cold stare of disapproval and a new G.I. Joe. It was put to me bluntly that "little boys don't play with Barbie dolls like little girls do," and that was that.

My father was a warm man grown cold through military service. Military culture adheres to strict standards on what is and isn't normal, and the troops are trained accordingly. My father was too young to fight in the Vietnam War, but if he'd been old enough, he would have volunteered to go. Instead he enrolled in West Point Military Academy, graduating in the class of 1976. He wanted to become a soldier like his father, who served as a pilot in World War II. Dad made military school sound fun with his tales of bar fights and hazings, all-night escapades with friends, and driving fast cars across the country end to end with no sleep. He was a skilled mechanic and had rebuilt two 1967 Jaguar XKEs in his mother's garage, crashing the first spectacularly.

I loved hearing these stories about his wild youth, but they became less and less frequent as he ascended in military rank. He was a hard, stoic man, and while he intimidated me, I was proud on the occasions when he would pick me up from school dressed in full fatigues, shiny black jump boots, and aviator sunglasses. People saluted my father when he walked by. He was known as Major Gabel, and he wouldn't have tolerated his oldest son wearing his wife's clothes.

My confusion over my interest in women's bodies and clothing followed me throughout elementary school. I'd see older women on the street and want to be as pretty as they were. At 8 years old, I caught an edited version of *Rosemary's Baby* playing on late night network TV. While most kids would shy away from the terror of the Roman Polanski film, I was drawn in by the beauty of Mia Farrow. Her hair was short and blond, chopped into a pixie cut, not dissimilar to my own. I knew what it felt like to have hair so short, so she made femininity real and attainable to me. I had no idea what kind of adult I'd grow up to be, but she gave me something to aspire to. Maybe, just maybe, I would look like her one day.

Music helped me cope with these feelings. I discovered 80s hair metal—bands like Poison, Warrant, and Bon Jovi. The first cassette I owned was Def Leppard's *Hysteria* album, purchased in a military PX because I liked the cover art of two faces screaming through a psychedelic triangle. But the band I became obsessed with was Guns N' Roses. Their music appealed to me because it felt dangerous. I was afraid of my parents seeing the liner note artwork. The look of the band, particularly that of wiry lead singer Axl Rose, excited me most because it was androgynous. Hair was big, clothes were tight, lines were blurred. I often couldn't tell if band members were boys or girls, and I liked that.

From hours spent poring over the photos in these albums, I knew I wanted to lead my own band. I started coming up with band names like "The Leather Dice" and writing them on the back of my jean jacket with a marker. I practiced stage moves by strumming along to songs using a tennis racket as a guitar. Eventually, I decided I needed to upgrade to a real one.

With money I'd saved mowing lawns, I ordered a $100 Harmony acoustic guitar from a Sears catalog. Waiting for it to arrive in the mail was excruciating. I already knew who I wanted to be, and I was eager to get started. My parents paid for lessons from an Army wife, but I got nothing out of them. Instead, I learned to play by ear, listening to my favorite albums and playing along to them. Like most kids who had their musical awakening in the 90s, I cut my teeth on Nirvana's "Smells Like Teen Spirit." The utter simplicity of that song taught countless rock hopefuls like me how to form power chords and annoy their parents with them. Frontman Kurt Cobain singlehandedly calloused a whole generation of tiny fingers with those opening notes.

For four years of my youth, ages 8 to 12, my family lived in Italy, and it was a dreamland to me. Our neighbors were a mix of Italian, British, Australian, and German families—soldiers and civilians. I practically lived outdoors there, running wild, playing war, exploring the acres of fruit orchards growing behind our house. I made friends in the neighborhood easily, but learned never to get too attached to other kids, as they moved often. One day you'd be playing catch with your friend, and the next, his father would be shipped halfway around the world. You were lucky if you got the chance to say goodbye.

My mother fully immersed herself in Italian culture, becoming fluent in the language and taking cooking lessons. She made a point of exposing my brother and me to as much of the country as she could. My father had a harder time adjusting. The military encouraged respect and interest in local culture, but to the Italians, United States military presence could never be seen as anything more than unwelcomed occupiers on Italian land.

Any preexisting problems my parents had in their marriage had been unknown to me, and only became apparent as they intensified with the escalation of the first Gulf War, Operation Desert Storm. Tensions were high for all military families stationed overseas. I was introduced to the concept of a "terrorist threat." Bomb sweeps of the school bus became part of my daily routine, and armed soldiers stood guard on the roof while teachers taught my classes. Armed Forces Network, the only English-speaking station we got on TV, played nothing but 24/7 war coverage.

My father saw his last chance to go to war and practically begged his commanding officers for the opportunity. But for whatever political and strategic reasons, he was never sent, instead left behind at the NATO post in Napoli while all his peers got to go play war. He gave me his chemical warfare gas mask one day to have as a toy, knowing he would never need to wear it in actual combat. He had reached a ceiling in the chain of military command and was deeply frustrated by it.

Communication between him and my mother disintegrated more each day. This gave way to yelling or fighting, usually in the mornings or evenings when he returned from base. Eventually they stopped speaking entirely.

Just before I turned 13, my parents separated for reasons that were never fully explained to me. My mother pulled me into her sewing room one day and told me that she planned on leaving and taking Mark with her. I was given the choice of coming with them or staying with my father. The situation made me feel terrible, but I chose her, because not doing so felt like betrayal. Instead I felt like I was betraying my dad. My mother has since told me that things would have ended sooner if she hadn't gotten pregnant with Mark.

The Army establishment frowns on divorce and the idea of women leaving officers, so moving out had been a long, arduous process for my mother. For two years, she had slept alone on the bed in Mark's room and I slept on a cot next to her, while Mark and our father shared the master bedroom. The mood in our house was tense. My father started withholding money from my mother and wouldn't pay for basic necessities. When my mother's car broke, he didn't fix it, essentially rendering her a prisoner of the house.

At night I heard the clacking of a keyboard coming from my father's office. He would sit in front of his computer for hours, typing something. He's never told me what he was working on all those nights, but I believed it to be some sort of journal, as if he was writing out the feelings he never spoke.

Eventually my mother took me and my brother to live with her mother, Grandma Grace, in her retirement condo in Naples, Florida, and my entire life changed. Suddenly I was a child of divorce, and my mother was a single parent to two boys, starting over after 13 years of marriage. She was without money, a job, a car, or a home. My father was left behind at his NATO station in Italy, where he was placed on suicide watch. My brother and I wouldn't see him again for a year.

I hated Florida immediately. It was hot and boring. We had spent the last four years dining on authentic Italian cuisine, but when we stepped off the plane at the Southwest Florida

Regional Airport, we had the option of celebrating our arrival at either Olive Garden or Domino's Pizza. No longer did my father's Army rank matter in school. This was civilian life. What mattered in Collier County was the size of your parents' bank account.

I didn't fit in with my classmates in my new high school, and none of them befriended me, which was fine because I didn't want to be their friend anyway. They weren't Army brats like me; they had all grown up together there, and I was the weird new kid. I was different. I wore United Colors of Benetton, and they wore Air Jordans. I rode a big cruiser bike with a basket, a hand-me-down from my grandma, while they all owned BMX stunt bikes. Even my teachers treated me like an outcast. In Italy, my teachers thought I was exceptional and would engage with me, placing me in the gifted programs. But in Florida, they treated me like I was invisible. I didn't know any other students in my class whose parents were divorced, and I felt like that was a stigma. Naples didn't feel like another temporary military assignment I'd need to briefly adjust to; it felt like it would be the rest of my life. I felt alone and trapped, and I just wanted my dad back.

As a newly single woman, my mother relied heavily on the church, making use of their after-school programs for me and Mark while she worked long shifts at a framing shop. My first three live musical performances were in front of church congregations in talent shows. I entered them with R.J. and Nick, two other kids in the youth group. We called our band the Black Shadows. While playing, I felt filled with the Holy Spirit, although I'm not sure anyone saw it in me. All three of these performances consisted of single cover songs: first an a capella rendition of Queen's "Bohemian Rhapsody," followed the next year by an acoustic version of John Lennon's "Imagine."

Finally, after ripping through Nirvana's "Heart-Shaped Box" as a fully electrified band, the church asked that I no longer participate. They also told my mother that they thought I was troubled after noticing the cut marks I'd made on my arms and legs, a habit I'd picked up to impress cute girls in school. I'd carve a crush's name into my shoulder, or make slashes on my forearm to win their attention. The pain was intense, but it paid off when a few girls took notice. Unfortunately, so did the youth ministers. The church paid for me to see a psychiatrist and told me not to come back until I received help. When a church turns you away, it feels as though God himself is rejecting you, saying you are damaged beyond His help.

I spent a lot of time at home. Fortunately, my grandmother's house had cable, and I passed the time by watching MTV. I stayed glued to the channel, hoping for the hosts to play another Nirvana or Pearl Jam video. When I grew bored, I would lock myself in the bathroom and try on my mother's dresses that were in the hamper. I'd stand there as long as I could, looking at myself in the mirror, wishing I was someone else, wishing I was her.

Who was "her"? She was the person I imagined myself to be, in another dimension, in a past life, in some dream. I had never heard of gender dysphoria; the idea that your psychological and emotional gender identities do not match your assigned sex at birth. I didn't have a name for the way I felt. No information was available, and there was no adult that I could trust with my secret. I thought I was schizophrenic, or that my body was possessed by warring twin souls: one male, one female, both wanting control.

I would look down at my body in a dress and blur my vision until it almost felt real. My eyes scanned upward, hoping to see her face, but I would only find an insecure teenage boy dressed in women's clothes. I'd do this until it was time to take the dress off and go through the motions of flushing the toilet and pretending to wash my hands before stepping back into reality.

I grew my hair down to my shoulders under the guise of rebellion and rock and roll, wanting to emulate the bands whose posters I tacked to my bedroom walls. But secretly I just wanted long hair like all the girls my age. My long hair and band T-shirts got me labeled a freak at school and led to fights. Someone was always waiting after class or on the walk home, ready to jump me. I was never a good fighter; I was too tall and lanky, already almost grown into the six-foot-two frame I'd eventually fill. I'd always end up bloodied and bruised.

One of my most violent encounters was with a member of the football team, who loved to bully kids like me, although I brought this one on myself by teasing him about shaving his legs. As if from a John Hughes movie, the jock threatened to kick my ass after school. "Three PM in the hallway," he said. "Be there or I'll find you." I showed up, but before I could even say a word or do anything, his friend charged up behind me and clocked the side of my head, knocking me to the ground. I landed next to some paint cans by a janitor's closet. I picked one up and started swinging with everything I had. I hit them as many times as I could, in between punches they landed on me while kids cheered on. An administrator came by and everyone scattered. I left the building and ran across the street toward the mall, while the jocks got in their car to hunt me down. My face swollen, I hid behind a dumpster in the parking lot until it got dark.

I soon lost the desire to go to class and became a pro at playing hooky. I left the house in the morning to walk to school as usual, but instead ducked behind a diner and smoked cigarettes until I was sure my mom had gone to work. Then I was free to sit at home wearing one of her dresses, sipping Kahlua and creams from the cabinet while watching soap operas. Getting drunk alone became a routine and was a natural predecessor to my interest in drugs.

Drugs were embedded in the culture in Naples. South Florida was an international point of entry for the U.S. drug pipeline. Missing their intended drop points, kilos would regularly fall out of the sky and wash up on shore into the arms of sheriff's deputies. It was easier for a kid my age to buy cocaine than alcohol. Hanging outside the mall on a Friday night smoking cigarettes got you in with the kind of kids who wanted to get fucked up, too. After cigarettes became a habit for me, I smoked weed and ate acid or psychedelic mushrooms, which could be easily harvested from farm fields after a summer rain. With the exception of huffing, I was willing to try anything I could get my hands on, and I always wanted more. I tasted cocaine for the first time at 13 years old, snorting lines in the bathroom of the public library, right off a copy of Jack London's *A Daughter of the Snows*.

Through experimentation, I noticed the way different drugs affected my dysphoria. When I smoked weed, what seemed like a fantasy became more real and I felt less panicked; time stood still. When I drank or did cocaine, I became numb, and I didn't care that I couldn't be her. All I wanted was another drink or another line. On psychedelics, though, not only could I fully become her, but I could fully detach from all reality.

After one year, my father's next assignment brought him back to America, in Fort Leonard Wood, Missouri, where he would eventually retire after his 20th year of his service and marry a woman almost 20 years his junior. It seemed obvious to me and Mark that she didn't want anything to do with kids, let alone the kids from her new husband's previous marriage. Dad didn't even tell us that he had gotten remarried. We learned by noticing that her last name had changed on the mail being sent to their house. Mark and I split our lives between school years in Florida and summers in Missouri, but neither of us were able to get our relationship with our father back on track after the divorce.

I hated Missouri almost as much as I hated Florida. My father's house was miles off base in a desolate spot in the middle of Mark Twain National Forest, where there was no cable, and therefore, no MTV. I wandered through those woods praying I'd stumble onto a field of marijuana growing, like I'd seen in drug busts on TV. With no other way to catch a buzz, I settled for stealing my dad's beers and highball glasses of schnapps after he went to sleep.

At my request, my dad built me a bedroom in the basement. Like my childhood forts, I liked the isolation it offered. The cavelike darkness let me sleep all day, and the privacy meant I could do whatever I wanted after everyone else had gone to sleep.

Restless at night, I would search through my dad's old military footlockers, looking at pictures and reading old letters. There were boxes from my father's past life; his half of the family possessions received in the divorce. In one of those boxes I found my mother's wedding dress. I spent all summer in that basement, dressed like a bride, and drinking Miller Lites while playing guitar or writing in my journal.

Journaling was something I'd picked up in third grade when my father was assigned to a month-long training exercise in Germany and had to pull me and Mark out of school. Because I was going to be missing so much class, my teacher told me to keep a journal and write about my traveling experiences every day. I wrote about visiting the Dachau concentration camp outside of Munich. Walking the grounds where thousands of Jewish people had been put to death by a deranged Nazi, I knew that the devil must be real. I also wrote about seeing my brother bolt into oncoming traffic and be struck by a delivery truck, which stopped directly on top of his legs. We spent the night in the hospital with him. He was shaken up, but fortunately his young bones did not break under the weight. The experience was traumatizing, but it taught me the value of expressing myself on paper. Its confessional nature was therapeutic. I came back from the trip, read these two entries in front of my class, and received an A on the assignment. I never stopped keeping a journal after that.

The only break in the monotony of Missouri was our trip to visit my grandparents' lake cabin in northeastern Pennsylvania, where I had an attic bedroom to myself. One night, I stumbled upon a sports almanac there. There was a two-paragraph article in it about Renée Richards, the professional tennis player who underwent a male-to-female sex change.

This was the first time I'd ever heard of such a concept. I could hardly believe it was really possible. In the sanctuary of the attic, I read those two paragraphs over and over. I wanted this so badly, but didn't know how to make it happen. All those sleepless nights praying to God for this one miracle never got me a word back. After everyone was asleep, in a moment of pure desperation, I turned to Satan.

There on a cot set up among boxes, beneath a single pull-string light bulb, I kneeled in front of the bed and took out a piece of paper, the sports almanac underneath for a hard surface, a bird feather for a pen, and my Swiss Army knife. I cut my thumb and dipped the end of the feather into the growing droplet, and started writing.

"I pledge my allegiance to the Dark Lord in exchange for..."

I vowed to do whatever he wanted. I offered my soul, anything in trade. I begged for Satan to please, please let me wake up a woman. Not a girl, but a fully grown woman; instant emancipation so that I could run away and escape it all. I had a full, intricate plan worked out in my head. I would wake up that next morning before the rest of my family and disappear into the woods, never to be seen again. I wrote out the contract and signed it in my own blood, but of course I never woke up the woman I wished to be.

Puberty arrived, and with it came a raging flow of testosterone. My body started changing, and I felt the peer pressure to have sexual experiences, the thought of which terrified me.

I don't know how I pulled off dating a senior as a sophomore, let alone one as beautiful as Tami. Still too young for a license, embarrassingly I had to ask my mom for the occasional drive to her house. Tami was sexually experienced, and I was not. She seemed out of my league. I had gotten a blowjob from one of the girls at church, and she had let me finger her, but I had never gone all the way. I was both terrified and relieved when Tami and I started dating, knowing that I would most assuredly lose my virginity to her.

Her alcoholic mother was passed out in the other room one night, and we were watching the early Angelina Jolie movie *Hackers* on the living room couch. Neither of us had any interest in the movie. I just sat there, nervously trying to think of a way to make a move, when she took me by the hand and led me into her bedroom, leaving the lights off. She pushed me down onto the bed and started taking her clothes off, and I followed suit. Once naked, she straddled me. This was it. This was the moment. I was going to have sex. My skin felt like it was on fire. I was so flushed with nerves, sweating bullets before any action even started. She put me inside of her and...ecstasy. I was reborn. I came within seconds.

"Before you cum, let's stop and put a condom on, yeah?" she whispered into my ear.

"Um...it may be a little too late for that..."

We dated for another four months before I broke up with her after she told me she slept with her ex-boyfriend. But those four months were like sex boot camp. She taught me how to fuck, telling me exactly what did and didn't feel good, stopping short of breaking out charts and graphs. I was fascinated by her body. I liked fucking just as much as I liked drugs, each of them their own escape.

The rush of pubescent hormones only amplified my dysphoria, and I grew even more angry and confused. Why did I desperately feel that I wanted to be a girl but at the same time have deep crushes on all the girls at school? I feared that I was gay. The thought of intimacy scared me. Could someone love me if they knew my secret? And would it really be true love if I kept this part of me from them? This mess of thoughts brought on my first memorable bout with depression, a mental illness present in both sides of my family. Grandma Grace, who never remarried after her husband died of a heart attack in 1964, would slip into depression and not get out of bed for days. We would admit her to the hospital for treatment, and she'd spend a month there, get released, and six months later, need to be admitted again. I felt like I understood her hopelessness.

While drugs and sex could reliably hold me over, my biggest distraction and relief from depression came when I discovered punk rock.

"You should give this album a listen," said Debbie, handing me a copy of *Dookie* by Green Day. Debbie and her husband, Sam, owned Offbeat Music, the only independent record store in Southwest Florida at the time. "This band is about to be huge," she assured me. "Get in before they sell out!"

Soon I caught Green Day's video for "Longview" on MTV's *120 Minutes*, a show I would stay awake every Sunday night to watch at the price of exhaustion on Monday morning. The video was everything Debbie had promised—punk slackers killing their suburban boredom by watching TV. The meta nature of this was not lost on me. One night, I saw an episode guest-hosted by Rancid's Tim Armstrong and Lars Frederiksen, two punks with foot-high mohawks, tattoos, and leather jackets completely covered in metal spikes. They looked like they were from another planet. I was immediately back at Offbeat the next day seeking out the albums by every band whose video they played. Each of those albums led me to discover other bands and opened up a whole new world of music—the Clash, X, Operation Ivy, the Ramones, NOFX, and an endless list of others.

Using my mom's razor and scissors, I cut my long hair and shaved the sides into a mohawk, spiking it up with Knox gelatin. I stole a pair of black Levis from the mall and ordered a Discharge shirt from a punk mail-order catalog. This, combined with black combat boots, became my uniform. I never changed or washed them. When holes developed in my jeans, I would simply sew punk patches over them. Inspired by a photo of the Germs' singer, Darby Crash, I stuck a safety pin through my ear and started collecting piercings—a few in my ears, one through my septum, two through my nipples, one through my dick. A thick chain connected to a padlock hung around my neck. None of this was ideal in the sweltering heat and daily rain of Florida, but I was willing to suffer for punk fashion.

Green Day was touring through Florida with a stop at a venue called the Edge in Orlando. A friend from class named Dustin Fridkin was also a Rancid and Green Day fan, and his dad bought us tickets and volunteered to drive us. In advance of the concert, we both dyed our hair green.

Standing in the audience waiting for the band to take the stage, the new Rancid album was playing over the house PA.

"What is this shit they're playing? I wish Green Day would hurry up and come out," griped the two girls standing in front of us. Dustin and I turned to each other and rolled our eyes. We were more in the know and thus cooler than they were.

When the band finally walked out, the floor in front of us instantly opened up into a violence I'd only heard rumor of—a circle pit. It was terrifying, but there was no question as to whether or not we were heading in. This was the last step in our initiation. Fists flew, bodies surfed overhead. No matter how many times we were spit out, we jumped back in until the show was over.

Waiting for Dustin's dad on the curb outside the venue, shirt collars torn, bloodied and bruised, green hair dye melted out of our hair and onto our faces, we had seen the future.

"We should start a punk band of our own!" I said.

Punk was the perfect outlet for a young outcast living in Naples. The city mainly comprised tourists and rich, white, elderly people. That was where the tax revenue came from, so that was who the city services catered to. Youth was preferably neither seen nor heard. There was nowhere to go and nothing to do, other than swim at the beach—and I hated the beach. After Tami and I broke up, I started seeing a girl named Jenn. I pawned the Mickey Mantle baseball card my dad had given me to buy bus tickets out of town for us. We only made it as far as the Greyhound station in Fort Myers, the next city north on I-75, before being picked up by the sheriff's department. My mom had reported me after coming home from work for lunch unexpectedly and finding the goodbye letter I'd left on the kitchen table. We were both grounded for weeks after that. I felt trapped and thought I'd never leave Naples alive.

Punk rock was a cathartic way to fight back against the town's bigotry—the asshole jocks at school who beat me up and called me a faggot, a church and God that turned me away and damned my soul, and teachers who wanted to erase my individuality. It was the nihilism and self-destructive nature of punk rock that I first latched on to. Live fast, die young. Then at 15, on the Fourth of July, I had a change of perspective. Punk politics that seemed only theoretical became all too real.

I was a scrawny, Sid Vicious–looking kid. I weighed 100 pounds soaking wet, a dirty, smelly trouble magnet who liked to run his mouth. I ran it to the wrong cops on the wrong day.

Looking for some friends on the boardwalk, I heard a voice from behind me, thick with authority. "Time to move along, son!"

I turned around to find two cops; one male, one female. The one who'd said it was the spitting image of Erik Estrada from *CHiPs*—same coiffed hairdo, same silver aviator sunglasses, one thumb hitched in his belt buckle, close to his gun, and the other hand pointing at me while barking orders. I walked away through the crowd of red, white, and blue-clad patriotic families, still in search.

"I already told you, son, it's time to move along!" he said when he found me again.

Before I could even give any lip back, my arms were twisted behind my back. I was led by the shoulder and slammed face-first onto the trunk of a Collier County sheriff's cruiser that had been baking in the summer sun all day. I kept bucking up off the sizzling hot metal and was slammed back down each time. Both officers held me down, spread my legs apart, and emptied out my pockets.

"You fucking Nazi pigs, you fascist fucking assholes! What the fuck are you arresting me for? Fuck you! Fuck you!!!" I shouted. The officer grabbed the back of my hair and slammed my head multiple times on the trunk, slapped handcuffs on me, opened the door to the cruiser, and threw me in the back as more cops showed up.

He looked down at me through the open window and I could see myself in the reflection of his sunglasses. "You're going to jail, you little fucker!" I mustered all the saliva I could in my mouth and spit it directly into his face.

The door was ripped back open and I was pulled out. I collapsed to my knees and was lifted by the elbows, a cop on each side. All my body weight leaned into my cuffed wrists and I kicked my feet out, flailing to hit whatever I could. Two more officers rushed over, each grabbing a leg. More backup continued to arrive. I was carried around the car into the street and thrown face-first to the ground. A boot on my head, a knee in my back. My ankles were zip-tied to my wrists. Hog-tied and defenseless, I was picked up like a suitcase and carried around while the pigs shared a laugh at my squirming.

When we arrived at the station, parked inside the jail receiving area, the back door opened by my knees and I heard a voice say, "I'm going to cut your ankles free now. If you kick me, I'm going to kill you."

Sitting alone in a cell waiting still to be processed for release, the Estrada look-alike entered and sat down in front of me. "Look at this face, you little asshole," he said, pointing to his smug grin. "Look at it good and never forget it. Oh yeah, you little shit, you're screwed, I got you, you're fucked. Remember this face as long as you live. I'm always coming for you."

Hours later, my mother posted bond. A reporter came to our house the next day and interviewed me for a story about whether police had gone too far in handling my arrest and if it bordered on brutality. My mother gathered all her savings and retained a lawyer for my defense.

I was tried as an adult on charges of resisting arrest with violence and battery on an officer, and ultimately convicted of both felonies. It came down to siding with a member of law enforcement or a punk teenager, and the court chose the law. I got off relatively easy with a summer of house arrest and 180 hours of community service, which I spent volunteering in the cardiac rehabilitation wing of the local hospital.

Once my probation-regulated drug testing sobered me up a bit, I realized that something inside me had changed. Suddenly the dick and fart jokes in the NOFX songs I'd grown to love seemed less appealing. Punk became more than mohawks and patches. I was pissed off. My arrest and conviction were a catalyst, politicizing my teenage mind, opening up new worlds of thought, and turning me on to anarchist philosophy. I had seen the way the system worked firsthand, and I knew I wanted nothing to do with it. The more I looked, I saw oppression and inequality happening all around me.

Fights at school were finding me more often and were becoming more intense. Most of my friends had already dropped out, and I was sick of getting my ass kicked every day. After the second time I ran away from home—this time only making it as far as Offbeat Music before being picked up by the cops—my mother told me I could drop out if I promised not to run away again. At 16, I threw my textbooks in a dumpster and washed my hands of school forever.

My mother got remarried to a gentle, goofy guy who was the polar opposite of my dad, and I made life hell for them. This wasn't new for her, of course. As in my toddler days, I was still "Tom Tom the Atom Bomb." In addition to my charge of resisting with violence, I picked up arrests for resisting without violence, possession of weed, carrying a concealed weapon (a thick bike chain, in case anyone tried to fuck with me), and the usual Friday night detentions by mall security. But mom was always there to bail me out, and I was always an ungrateful little shit.

She even helped me buy a car once I got my license, a 1976 Buick LeSabre. Soon after, I was driving around with some friends one night, and got in a car chase with some football players in a red Mazda Miata, no match for the 350 V8 under the Buick's hood. After I sideswiped them into a ditch, I thought I had lost them, but they followed me to my house. I stored a machete under my car seat, never knowing when it might come in handy. I grabbed it, hopped out, and started wailing on their hood with it. Their doors flew open, and they charged me. They had called my bluff, since I wasn't going to kill them with a machete. My friends ran toward my house, so I bolted after them. My mother was awakened by all the noise. She rushed out onto the lawn wielding a baseball bat to scare off my attackers. Everyone was screaming at each other until my mother suddenly froze, grabbed her chest, and dropped to her knees. The guys were so shocked by this that they got back in their car and sped off. Meanwhile, my stepdad and I rushed her to the emergency room. The doctor told us it was a stress-induced heart attack. I literally gave my mother a heart attack.

She became liberal with my drinking after that, saying that if I was going to do it, then she'd prefer I did so at home so I wouldn't end up in fights or in jail. My bedroom, which had a separate entrance, became a hangout for all of my friends.

By 1997, I was 16 going on 17, and was falling deep into the English peace-punk scene—the Mob, Zounds, Poison Girls, and, of course, Crass, who remain my favorite band to this day. I also took an interest in Profane Existence, a Minneapolis-based anarcho-punk collective which was associated with smaller, more politically vocal bands like Man Afraid, Civil Disobedience, Destroy, and State of Fear. I was going to shows, reading fanzines, and collecting records.

My interest in these bands had as much to do with their sound and their look as it did with their do-it-yourself, or DIY, ethos and anarchist politics. It wasn't about money for them. They sought revolution and freedom, and they approached making music as an act of political protest. These bands wanted to empower their audiences. I studied their lyrics, and, like them, I was fine with starving for my ideals. Fuck MTV and fuck major labels. Fuck commercial art. Fuck the whole capitalist system! I wanted nothing to do with any of it. All of these new records and cassettes I was discovering made music seem accessible in a way it had never been before.

I'd had some experiences playing in bands here and there. Dustin had a guitar and a basement we could practice in—a rarity in Florida due to the state's high water table—and my mother had bought me a Fender P Bass from a pawn shop for my birthday. We started a band called the Adversaries, playing our biggest out-of-town show in Gainesville, Florida, at the Hardback, a legendary punk dive bar that would close within months. After the Adversaries dissolved, I played bass in a grindcore band called Common Affliction, which was really just an elaborate excuse to eat tacos with friends.

These bands were always just for fun and weren't intended to go anywhere. But I wanted to take writing music seriously. I realized that since no one else was going to do it for me, I should just take it into my own hands. So I set a simple goal for myself: I would write and record 10 songs.

At the time, I didn't have an electric guitar. If I remember correctly, I had traded it to my old drummer for weed. So I recorded the songs in my bedroom using my acoustic guitar and an electric bass with a four-track my mother had given me and some stolen microphones. I designed the cover of the cassette, too: a cut-and-paste job of a Vietnamese prisoner of war with his arms bound behind his back. Across the top, I scrawled two words capturing my teen angst; words that would map out the next two decades of my life, words that would set the tone for my career in music and become inseparable from my own name. I called it Against Me!.

After mastering the fine art of scamming free photocopies out of the local Kinko's—a rite of passage for any DIY punk—I folded each up and inserted the booklets into the plastic cases of the cassettes I had dubbed until I had a small stack of Against Me! tapes. All my former bandmates hated the songs, and with good reason: they were fucking terrible. But I loved the process. I loved creating something. I loved putting something I made out into the world and being in full control of the art. This was mine alone. So on the high of this success, I set the next logical goal for myself: I would play one show.

From my experiences with the Adversaries and Common Affliction, I already knew that performing in front of people with a band was nerve-wracking enough. The thought of doing it alone was downright terrifying. I figured I'd play one show and get over it. So I got myself booked at a vegan café in Fort Myers called Raspberries, a daytime show on an open-air patio. With a five-song set list, in front of 20 disinterested people comprising mostly the staff and other performers, no stage to stand on, one shaky chord after another...very unceremoniously, Against Me! was born.

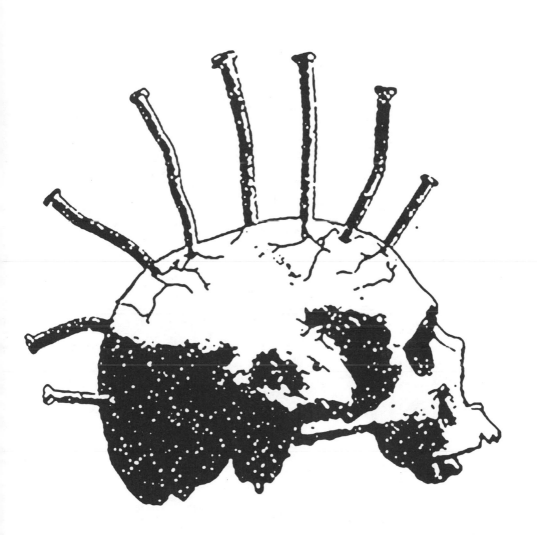

Kevin Mahon was a kid I'd met outside a movie theater where he was getting bullied, knocked around, and called a faggot. I stuck up for him, and we became friends. He was three years younger than me, which is a wide gap at 16, but there weren't enough punks in the scene to be choosy about who your friends were. Even though he was young, I could tell that Kevin had vision. A fellow dropout, he also had ample free time during the day when everyone else was at school.

I had overcome the stage fright about playing solo, but realized it was more fun to play music with other people. I was itching to make another tape, this time with a drummer. Since Kevin didn't have a full drum kit, we built one out of the few pieces he had and some pickle buckets found in a dumpster. I put an emphasis on not wanting to sound like any other band.

"You shouldn't play with any cymbals," I told him. "What drummer plays with no cymbals? Besides, you sound better without them. I want only primal beats, and the cymbals drown out my acoustic guitar."

Kevin and I practiced every day, and we had chemistry like I had never experienced. It was as if we could read each other's minds, and we always knew exactly what each other wanted in a performance. I would come up with an idea, and Kevin would make it better. I'd usually start with lyrics, filling up a journal page until I had enough for a couple of verses and a chorus. Then I'd string together a few chord progression ideas and bring it all to Kevin, and we'd shape a song out of it. Kevin and I practiced in my bedroom every day of the week, for as many hours as my mother could stand.

There was nowhere to play in Naples, and we were considered a joke band at the few places there were, so we busked on street corners for spare change, two hippie punks with buckets and acoustic guitars. We didn't care that no one got it. I was confident in our aim and our intentions, and knew that if there wasn't an audience for us in Southwest Florida, we would find one elsewhere.

Beyond our musical kinship, Kevin and I became best friends. Neither of us had many other friends, and once we found each other, we didn't need any. We were an inseparable duo, like if Beavis and Butt-head were anarchist activists. Kevin became a constant presence at my house, free to come and go as he pleased. I had two beds in my room; one mine, one his. We both became vegan and started a local chapter of Food Not Bombs, a movement dedicated to sharing vegan meals as a means of protesting war and poverty.

After practice, we'd hit the town on the warpath for destruction. In the name of class warfare we'd sneak into golf courses and tear the grounds up by digging into the dirt with our hands, rolling up the whole greens, and throwing them into the lagoon, leaving nothing but a dirt patch and a hole behind. When we needed money, we'd steal squeegees from gas stations and use them to fish coins out of the fountains around town.

There was a sexual tension between us, too. When I first met him, he was a little goth kid, wearing black lipstick and fishnet sleeves, but after we started hanging out, he began to emulate my style and became punk. I thought he might have a crush on me. We were drinking in my room one hot summer night, and I stood up to flip the record on the turntable. I turned back to find Kevin had taken off his shirt and was opening and adjusting his pants, giving me a look that I interpreted as inviting. Maybe it was just wishful thinking on my part, but I thought Kevin maybe wanted to fuck me. I thought I maybe wanted to fuck Kevin back. This was confusing because we both liked girls, and it made me wonder if I was gay. There was an awkward silence in the room, and then, panicked, I turned back to my records, and nervously started talking about Crass. We both pretended like it never happened.

With all the time we spent together, we were able to write enough songs to record another cassette. We titled it *Vivida-Vis!* And with that, we aimed to book our first tour.

Since the internet and cell phones were not yet an omnipresent wealth of information for traveling bands, I relied heavily on pen pals I'd made through zines and my copy of *Book Your Own Fucking Life*, a resource guide published by the people at *Maximum Rocknroll*, a long-running and widely distributed monthly fanzine dedicated to the underground punk scene. I mailed *Vivida-Vis!* out to other punks throughout the country, asking for a plate of food and a place to rest. I started hearing back and mapped out a month-long tour of the East Coast in the spring of 1999 for the two of us. Fortunately, my girlfriend at the time, Alana, a punk rock girl with SHIT tattooed across her wrist, had two things any broke, aspiring band needs: a van and a debit card. We were golden.

The first place we ended up playing on tour was an open mic night in Decatur, Georgia. The other performers were your average singer/songwriter-types—think Jewel but less Alaskan, Jack Johnson but less surf—and then there was me and Kevin, screaming about anarchist politics in people's faces. There was a bewildered silence after we finished, and we most definitely did not win that night's prize money.

We showed up hours late to our second show, a punk house in Asheville, North Carolina, called the Pink House. The organizer, Aaron Cometbus, scolded us and said we could only play six songs to make room for the many other bands on the bill, which was fine with us because it didn't even cut our set list in half. We played through a busted PA and a crappy amp, but we rocked the shit out of those six songs. The people watching us went off, dancing and clapping along. This was the first time that people had ever danced or sung along to us while we played. What a high, what a rush. It felt like our music was actually connecting with people. We hung out with everyone afterward, drinking 40-ounce malt liquor, the preferred drink of choice in punk culture after Rancid popularized it in their "Salvation" video, and also because it was incredibly cheap. We felt like we'd truly arrived.

Most of the other shows on the tour fell through. The places we did end up playing were squats, houses, and garages. We brought a boombox with us, and after every show, we dubbed more copies of the demo tape for anyone who wanted one. We started to catch on, especially in Florida's political punk scene. We ended up making a thousand copies. We also killed Alana's van and drained her bank account in the process. She dumped me shortly after the tour ended.

I loved being on the road because it kept my mind away from feelings of dysphoria. This would become a common theme throughout life—binging and purging. At home, boredom and curiosity led me to sit around in dresses, but on tour, I could forget about it and avoid temptation for weeks at a time. Then I would return home, and the urge would hit me all over again.

The touring experience galvanized us, and when we got back, Kevin and I immediately started work on another EP. One of the pen pals I'd made was this crusty punk rock Jewish kid named Jordan Kleeman, from Pikesville, Maryland. Jordan was part of a collective of fellow anarchists that ran a small DIY punk label called Crasshole Records. Before actually meeting them, I imagined them as hardened class warriors, living on the fringes and smashing the state. In reality, they were smashing the state from Jordan's mother's living room couch while drinking sodas and eating Utz potato chips from her pantry. Like us, they loved the band Crass, and, also like us, they were assholes—thus the label's name. Eventually, he changed the name to Sabot, in reference to the wooden shoes that French factory workers threw into gears to sabotage production during the Industrial Revolution.

The label put out our first vinyl release, a 12-inch EP. They printed 500 copies, and, due to a recording error that went unnoticed before going to press, it ended up sounding like complete shit. Bands in this scene were known for having a lo-fi feel, but this sounded like it was coming out of a speaker that had been taken out back and beaten with a sledgehammer. We had no choice but to sell them, though, since we had to recoup the money for the pressing. I absolutely hated it. Still, some people out there will tell you it's the best thing we've ever done.

One of the copies landed in the hands of James Bowman. I had met James on the first day of freshman year at Naples High School. Sporting a Gwar T-shirt and a green mohawk, he went running past me down a hallway, being chased by two rednecks. "Who the fuck was that punk?" I thought. By lunch, we were good friends.

We had lined up a second tour, and James offered to buy

all the guitar strings for us, so he was in. Always ahead of the curve when it came to gear, James owned a Gibson Les Paul and a Marshall amp, literally amplifying our sound. He also had a girlfriend, Jenny, who he surprised us with and brought along for the ride. For the next month and a half, my Buick was a cramped traveling home for the four of us: Kevin, James, Jenny, and me. That car rolled down the road on a cloud. It was a boat. Tons of trunk space, but not great on gas. It did, however, have a working cassette tape deck and a CB radio.

The tour varied from city to city. In Chicago, we were humbled to play the legendary venue Fireside Bowl, where we felt like a legitimate band. Then the next night, we'd end up playing in Des Moines in some kid's parents' guesthouse where the audience ran at full force and launched themselves into the walls while we played.

It was the tail end of the 90s punk scene, where activism and anarchist politics were still prevalent. In a couple of years, Homeland Security would strike fear into the hearts of punk protesters after 9/11. After that, the scene forever changed and became more complacent. Really, it was the perfect time for our songs like "Baby, I'm an Anarchist" to connect with people.

Shows fell through all the time, and there was a 50/50 chance that anyone would actually show up to the ones that didn't get canceled. We didn't care either way. Touring was about travel and adventure, going to places you had never been and learning who you were in the process. We were green as a touring band, and I hated being green. I was determined to change that.

We slept on floors or outside under the stars. For money, we begged for spare change outside shopping malls, or expensive camera batteries were stolen from Walmart and returned to buy tents with the money. We picked up hitchhikers and forced them to listen to our punk cassettes. When a block of shows fell through after Fargo, we spent a week camping in Montana in the woods outside a mining ghost town. When another stretch of shows fell through on the West Coast, we spent a week sleeping on the beach outside Santa Cruz in a hut made of driftwood. We had driven overnight to reach the coast. It was my first time that far west. I wanted to touch the Pacific. I slept on the hood of the car, and woke with the sunrise to see the great blue ocean expanding before me.

The only way we ate was by begging for food. Specifically, we had discovered that Kentucky Fried Chicken had a store policy that if you went to the counter and told the cashier you were hungry and had no money, they would serve you at least some biscuits and gravy on the house. Most of the time this approach worked. We found it to be successful in other restaurants, too. Maybe it was because the employees realized that if they didn't feed us, we weren't going to leave, and then they'd have a bunch of smelly punk kids to deal with.

We were selling a few records, however awful they sounded, and it seemed like everywhere we went, we picked up at least a couple fans. Whatever money was made was put into the gas tank to get us farther down the road.

The Buick's engine blew up on the drive back to Florida after the last show of the tour, loyal to the last mile. We came back from our conquest of the United States penniless, jobless, and homeless, but we'd had the time of our lives. We all scattered in our own directions to find places to live. Kevin moved in with his girlfriend, and James went to visit his sister in St. Petersburg one weekend and never came back. The future for the band looked bleak.

My mom said I could come back home and stay for as long as I needed, but moving back to Naples wasn't an option. I had made it out alive; there was no way I was going back. I would make Gainesville work. Somehow I was going to make the band work, too. I started crashing at a termite-infested punk house in an industrial area just south of downtown Gainesville dubbed the 911 House as the address was 911 SE 4th Street. By punk standards, it was a mansion. All available space had been converted into bedrooms, so on any given night, there would be 15 to 20 people sleeping under the roof, and sometimes even a few people on top of it. The house had an open-door policy for touring bands, train hoppers, drifters, and travelers. All wayward souls were welcome to crash. To kick in my $100 share of the rent, I sold my plasma at the blood bank and picked up part-time work as a screen printer, making shirts for bank fundraising events or kids' soccer jerseys. On my lunch break, I would walk over to the college, where Hare Krishnas served food in exchange for donations, which to me meant a free lunch.

Every night was a drunken party in the 911 House. We ran a bowling lane down the hallway and smashed a bowling ball into beer bottles at the other end. Bonfires raged in the backyard. Punk bands played in the dining room. If there was ever any food in the kitchen, it had been found in a dumpster or stolen. It wasn't uncommon to find someone drunkenly fucking or masturbating in the living room, or passed out naked on the couch. Scabies outbreaks happened regularly. One of the three people I shared a room with kept a small arsenal of assault rifles and handguns in the closet, which were taken out on only the most drunken occasions and fired at the metal sign posted in the field across the street, which warned: DO NOT COME IN CONTACT WITH PLANT OR ANIMAL LIFE. EXPERIMENTAL TOXIC WASTE SITE.

Gainesville is a college town. After the bars let out and the crowds of drunk meathead jocks had gone back to their fraternity houses, I would wander the downtown streets, staring longingly at the dresses on display in storefront windows, wishing that they were mine and that I had the body to fill them. All I wanted was to be one of the pretty college girls I saw around town. I started stealing a roommate's birth control pills and taking them to see if they would affect my dysphoria, but all I got were violent stomachaches. That, and the realization that I would have no idea what to do if breast tissue were to actually develop made me discontinue use.

In August, most leases were up in the college condos in Gainesville, and the graduates moved back home. Dumpsters were filled to the brim with their discarded belongings. You could find anything in there—TVs, furniture, video games, stereos. Hell, I found money; jars of loose change just tossed in the trash. From dumpster diving, and stealing from roommates' laundry, I amassed a small collection of women's clothes which I stored in my room, along with a wig I'd stealthily purchased from a beauty store.

By then, I had heard a few more stories about men medically transitioning into women, though mostly in sensationalized "sex change" tabloid headlines. I had also viewed a VHS copy of the borderline snuff film *Faces of Death*, a video compilation of actual human deaths, animal attacks, plane crashes, and executions, set to a soundtrack of death metal music, which also featured a full view cut-by-cut recording of a male to female sexual reassignment surgery. Though absolutely terrifying, this also fascinated me.

Even at the 911 House, there was no one I felt I could confide in with my secret about my gender confusion. Sex politics and queer culture were openly discussed in the radical activist punk scene, but gender identity was still a taboo. The acceptance and open-minded politics were part of what drew me to it. Show spaces were supposed to be open to everyone regardless of age, race, class, sex, or sexual preference, but for the most part it was just white kids oblivious to the privilege they came from. It also became clear to me that while these were the politics heralded by the scene, often they were not actually practiced.

Whenever the chance arose to put my dresses on behind a locked door in the 911 House, I would jump at it. If I didn't have privacy, I would sit on the curb in front of the house alone, chain-smoking rolled cigarettes while drinking, my lips turning black from the constant opening of the painted screw-top bottle. I'd sit and drink and write in my journal.

August 10, 2000--Gainesville, FL

I pull a dress down over my shoulders, following it down my body with my hands. I turn off the light. The lace is exciting to touch. Thigh-high black pantyhose held up by a black garter belt. Black silk panties hiding everything I want to forget exists. Fresh from the shower, my skin is clean and young, hairless on the chest and stomach. There is nothing virgin about me.

A matching black bra from Victoria's Secret wrapped around my chest, hooked in the back, holds rolled-up socks in place as my breasts. I have perfected this technique over time. Socks work the best. They don't bounce when you walk, there's no weight, but they look real in form. With the bra tight enough and the skin of my chest lifted and jammed just right, I have something like cleavage.

The door to my bedroom is shut and locked. I have double and triple-checked. I

light up a joint and sit down on the edge
of my bed, cross my legs. I inhale long
and slow. The high hits, I light a cigarette and suddenly become real. I become
her.

By the time I finish my cigarette, my
eyes have adjusted to the dark. I stand
up and look down at my body. Beautiful
under the kindest light. I walk back and
forth across the room. The feel of pantyhose covering my legs, the way the dress
brushes the back of my thighs as I walk.
These small sensations intoxicate me with
want.

My broad shoulders, big hands, Adam's
apple, the stubble breaking through on my
chin, my big ears, the cock tucked between
my legs, all of these things cease to
exist here in the dark of this room. I
dare not speak to ruin the illusion.

The high always reaches a peak. On the
comedown, reality starts to kick back in.
I realize the time again. The sun's always
rising in the sky somewhere. Time to
undress and face the day.

I tell myself every time that it's the
last time. I swear, just this one last
time and then never again.

Deep, deep down inside of me I know
that I am not a mistake. I do not feel
sick. I do not feel like a pervert. I am
not gay. I am not a fag. I am not a drag
queen. I am not a tranny. I am not a

transsexual. I am not transgender. I am
just her, a daughter, a sister, someone's
girlfriend, just like all the other pretty
college girls on campus.

———————

August 23, 2000--Gainesville, FL

Quiet night on the curb. Rolling tobacco
and Hurricane Malt Liquor. It's been three
days now since I started taking the birth
control pills I found in the bathroom. I'm
not sure whose they were, but they definitely weren't being used. I can't tell
if I feel anything. What will happen if I
keep taking these? Will I grow breasts? I
want to grow breasts. I want to know what
would it be like to know my body as a
girl.
What would it feel like to wear this
dress? What would it feel like to have a
boy take this dress off of me? What would
the weight of breasts being released from
a bra feel like; to have my nipples kissed
and sucked? What would it be like to be
aroused? What would it feel like to run a
finger across my cunt? What would it be
like to penetrate myself with that finger and feel my own wetness? What would
it feel like to have a boy touch me? What
would it be like to have my hips held
firmly? What would it be like to spread my

legs for a boy? What would it be like to have a boy cum inside of me? What would it feel like to be loved?

There are times when I can push the thought out but it always comes back. What if I were to pursue it? What if I were to have electrolysis to remove my facial hair? What if I started taking hormones? What if I had surgeries, my face, breast implants, tracheal shave? Bottom surgery too? Not that I could ever afford it. I can barely afford cigarettes right now. Would I ever be a pretty girl? Would I be happy as an ugly girl? Would anyone ever accept me as a girl? I could never have a child. These thoughts kill me.

Would it ever be enough?

I met Danielle at Common Grounds, a coffee shop by day and music venue by night. She had to buy me drinks since I was only 19. I didn't know anything about her or where she was from, just that something about her radiated in a way that called to my heart. Already a mother at 22, she still lived with the child's father, her ex-boyfriend, in an apartment above a crack den. I came over one night and asked her to take a bike ride with me. We rode out to Paynes Prairie, careful not to wake sleeping alligators along the swamp trails. Walking out into the clearing from the trees, I turned to her and saw her face, gray in the moonlight, almost light blue, and fell in love instantly.

I had gotten a job training as an auto mechanic as part of a Christian-run charity program that helped dropouts like me get

GEDs and training for eventual placement working in a real garage. Sometimes late at night, Danielle and I would break into the junkyard at my work and fuck in the cars. It felt like magic to hold a warm naked body against my own, and hers was ever so fragile.

In between sneaking off to desecrate the back seats of abandoned GTOs, I kept writing songs. The band booked our first proper recording session at Goldentone Studio in town to record a five-song EP called *Crime as Forgiven by . . . Against Me!*. Jordan took care of the cost of the session, and then had the songs pressed as a seven-inch. A DIY punk label from Bloomington, Indiana, called Plan-It-X Records agreed to put out the CD version, since Jordan couldn't afford to do both.

I was so hungry for the road, eager to go to all the places that I'd never been. I spent that Florida winter with Danielle, dreaming about touring while working on cars, going to classes, slowly saving up money to buy a van.

James hadn't been part of the recording of *Crime*, but he joined us on the tour we booked to support it. We also enlisted Dustin to play bass. In my mind, I will always think of James, Kevin, Dustin, and myself as the classic Against Me! lineup, if one wanted to believe in such a thing. There was no band like us at the time, mixing acoustic and electric punk sounds. That version of Against Me! spawned a long lineage of imitative folk-punk bands that followed, for better or usually worse.

It seemed overkill to load the van up with a thousand copies of *Crime*, but to our amazement, we sold all of them over the course of the tour. At three bucks each, we had enough money to buy gas and even some beer now and then. I noticed a shift on this tour. We'd show up to play somewhere and there would actually be an audience waiting. Word of Against Me! had started to spread.

While the tour was a new high for us, it ended with us upside down in a ditch. We were driving home from the final show in Bloomington, the last one the four of us would ever play together. Just north of Atlanta, we'd stopped at a Wendy's drive-thru and merged back on to 1-75, southbound. I was driving, James was riding shotgun, and we were the only two wearing seat belts. As soon as I saw the semi's headlights in the rearview mirror, I knew it was too late. The truck clipped the left side of the back of the van, causing us to skid and the driver's side tires to blow. We rolled, I'm not sure how many times. I only saw the French fries and Frosty hovering weightlessly in midair in front of me, as if we were floating through the zero gravity of space for a moment, then violently darting forward and exploding against the inside of the windshield. When we landed, all I could hear were gasps of panic from my friends. Kevin was the first one out, and he pulled us out one by one. We all walked away, glad to be alive, but the van was fucked and so was our gear. That moment will stay with me forever. For all I know, we died in that accident and everything since has been just a dream.

After we divided up the insurance money from the accident, we had a falling-out of sorts. Kevin decided he wanted to quit the band to go train-hopping with his girlfriend. I took his decision personally—probably more personally than I should have. Without Kevin, I didn't see a future for Against Me!, and I was crushed. I felt like he had broken up with me.

Left with no band, I had more time to spend with Danielle. In my mind, my future was set—I was going to be a mechanic, I was going to be a man. Just six months after we'd started dating, we were married. She proposed to me in a Pan-Asian restaurant in front of friends. I couldn't really say no. I was in love with her, but also terrified about the fact that she was already a mother. To me, that meant instant domestication.

I bought $75 silver rings from the Gainesville shopping mall, and we made it official at the county courthouse. We rented a small house and bought a 1970 Chevelle with my share of the insurance money from the van accident. We were trying to be a family: husband and wife and all that bullshit.

She was working as a waitress in a bar called the Top and got me a job checking IDs at the door. I was only 20. The owners didn't know I was underage, so I had to be ruthless with my authority. I never let anyone slide and even started taking pleasure in busting kids who presented fake IDs. A free meal, free beer all night, and I got to hang out and talk shit with my friends. The best job I ever had.

Dustin and I were keeping our eyes open for a new drummer to replace Kevin and were also recording another seven-inch for Sabot. Since it was just the two of us, it ended up being a five-song acoustic EP. Both this release and *Crime* were well received in the punk scene, getting glowing reviews in *Maximum Rocknroll* and all the other prominent zines. People were listening to the records, and we were getting a lot of positive feedback about what we were doing. Even though there really was no real band to speak of, the name Against Me! was gaining traction. Local punks were starting to give me compliments around town and would ask when we were playing again. One of those punks was Warren Oakes.

I'd known Warren from the Florida activist scene. He was from Sarasota. All of the radical activists who ran Food Not Bombs chapters in Florida would meet up every month in a different city and talk about what was going on in their community. We'd organize May Day events, activist training camps, Youth Liberation conferences, and protests. Many gallons of homebrew were downed, and many campfire songs were sung.

Most of the gatherings would devolve into a campfire "Depends party," named after the adult diapers, where people would dress up in nothing but a diaper and then proceed to piss or shit themselves for a laugh. If I was drunk enough, I would hang my chain wallet from my dick piercing and swing it around for a party trick. Everyone was all about non-monogamy. In other words, it was an orgy.

Warren was a year younger than I was, but I assumed he was a decade older when we first met because of his huge beard. He had this hippie-punk thing going on—dreadlocks, no shoes, dirty. I mean, we were all dirty, but Warren was dirti*er*. I admired Warren's politics, and still do. He has a kind heart and a gentle soul, and he treats people fairly.

He told me how much he appreciated what Dustin and I were doing, and I told him how badly I wanted to play with a drummer again. We made plans to meet up and try playing together. His feel behind the drums was significantly different than Kevin's, and nothing like the chemistry I wanted, but he was the best option. Warren's style completely changed the sound of Against Me!. He was a technically better drummer, but he played with cymbals in his kit and half as much heart. He also didn't have the same musical influences, so we didn't have common references to work with. I had to adapt my arsenal of songs and my songwriting process to his style. Songs didn't come as easily. But slowly, over the course of a long fall in Gainesville, we put together 11 songs with the intention of recording a full-length LP. Most of the songs were reworked from preexisting Against Me! releases, with only three written and arranged by the four of us.

In December 2001, four years after I recorded Against Me!'s first demo tape alone in my bedroom, I stepped into Goldentone with James, Dustin, and Warren. In two days, for the cost of $800, we recorded the band's debut album. Once again, I designed the cover, cut-and-paste-style with an X-Acto knife and glue stick: the band's name in huge red letters behind a black-and-white outline of my former childhood hero, Axl Rose.

Punk had taught me to hate bands like Guns N' Roses and

everything they represented—the greed and the commercialism, the excess and the egos. That world was utter bullshit to me now. Those bands had done it their way, and now it was time for me to do it mine.

Of course, what no one tells you when you're young and arrogant is that you eventually grow up to become the thing you hate. Or if they do tell you, you're too cocky to listen. Decisions aren't always cut-and-dried, and I would have to learn that lesson the hard way. But in the righteous punk arrogance of my youth, I wanted this album to stand in opposition to the corporate-owned music industry. I wanted it to light a fire, establishing an ethos and a set of principles that not only we could live by, but all bands that came after us.

I aimed to take my guitar, travel the world with it, and reclaim rock and roll, city by city. So I came up with a title and wrote it in the bottom corner of the cover. *Against Me! Is Reinventing Axl Rose.*

3. WE'RE NEVER GOING HOME

No Idea Records didn't have high expectations when they released *Reinventing Axl Rose* in March 2002, as evidenced by their modest first printing of 1,100 LPs. But we sold through the run pretty quickly. And then the next printing. And the next. To date, it has sold over 200,000 copies worldwide, and it is the bestselling album in the label's history.

Even though No Idea was an independent record label, owned by a husband and wife in Gainesville, I started to hear rumblings that some punks weren't pleased with our decision to branch out from the DIY scene we'd started in. Punks are particular like that. Any hint that you might actually be making a few bucks off of your art and they're ready to come after you with pitchforks. It wasn't a personal decision to leave Plan-It-X. The label owner didn't even have a phone number to reach him. Occasionally, he would mail me a box of our CDs, and that was pretty much the extent of our communication. As the band grew, we needed more support than he could offer.

Either way, I was overjoyed to finally be receiving any validation, and thankful to not be eating out of a dumpster anymore. At 21, I was working at the hippest bar in town, playing in the coolest band in town, and driving a muscle car. It was an absolute prime. Then my wife got pregnant.

The pregnancy was not planned. I was starting to see possibilities opening up for the band while also starting to feel more and more confined by the relationship. I felt guilty about it, but I wanted to tour. I didn't want to be changing diapers for the rest of my life. She asked what I thought we should do, and I told her that while I would ultimately support whatever decision she made, I didn't think we should have the baby. We could barely support the child she already had with a now-absent father. We were struggling to pay our $500 monthly rent. I was at home watching her kid during the day while she pulled waitressing shifts, and then I'd head to the bar to work through the night.

I wasn't sure what her true feelings about the pregnancy were, other than being certain that she resented me for the way I felt about it. She started drinking pennyroyal tea in an attempt to terminate the pregnancy. When that didn't work, she had a group of friends give her a home abortion, a "menstrual extraction." She didn't tell me until after it had already happened.

Although all of the women involved in the extraction were going to school to become midwives, they had little experience with that sort of procedure. There was a clinic in town that she could have gone to, and we had the money to pay for it. I was still willing to have the baby. I was blown away by how irresponsible I felt she had been, putting herself in danger like that. What if something had happened? What about her daughter? I was further hurt that she did it without telling me. Then she made a zine detailing her experience and distributed it around town for all of our friends to see. It was almost too much humiliation for my male ego to handle. I took on more work shifts just to stay out of the house as much as possible.

I would close the Top every night with the bartender, C.C. She was eight years older than me, married with a kid. Her face was beautiful while still carrying a natural "fuck you" expression, which scared the hell out of me. She dyed her already jet-black hair even blacker, and wore it short at her chin. The upper halves of her arms were covered in tattoos; an angel on one side, the devil on the other. We got to know each other while I mopped the floors and she counted out the register and restocked the bar.

We were both unhappy in our marriages, neither of us really wanting to go home at the end of our shifts, so we'd draw out the time as long as we could, sometimes not leaving until after the sun had come up. C.C. would pour drinks. Her singles were triples. We'd shoot a couple games of pool, down a few pints, and do a couple more lines of blow, although C.C. preferred to shoot her cocaine. She would play all her favorite songs for me on the jukebox, and I'd play all of mine for her. She loved Springsteen, and I forced Bob Dylan on her. Late nights closing the bar with C.C. helped to avoid the misery waiting for me at home. We got high together, instead of getting high alone.

It wasn't enough to stay out of the house; I wanted to stay out of Gainesville. I put my focus on the band as a sure escape from the town. We booked a summer tour; our first with an actual full-length album to promote. We were drawing more people than most of the bands we played with, though I was still insistent we maintain our anti-capitalist stance, and split any cash equally among all the bands playing each show. We still made enough to pay rent when we came back.

Dustin waited until the tour was almost over to break the

news: he decided he wanted to go back to college and would be leaving the band after the tour ended. I understood his reasons, but was still sad to see him go. We had been playing in bands together since we were 13 years old, and I knew this was an end of those times. We were down a bassist, right when our momentum was starting to build. But by a stroke of serendipity, I got a random email.

"Kick the bass player out of your band and let me join," Andrew Seward joked in the email.

"It's funny you should say that…" I wrote back.

Andrew was a stranger, really. We had only crossed paths twice before. He lived in Murfreesboro, Tennessee, and played in a band called Kill Devil Hills, with whom we had once played a show in Tallahassee. He had stage presence, and I liked the way he danced, always smiling and full of energy. He was in without a tryout. I told him that all he had to do was move to Gainesville and buy a bass amp. He'd made a strong enough impression on me the couple of times we had met that I instinctively knew this was the right decision.

Our first tour together was awkward initially. I was spending hours in a van with people I hardly knew, with the exception of James. I missed Dustin and Kevin immediately. It still felt like such a strange thing to be playing songs without Kevin, my musical kindred spirit. Against Me! started to adopt a new personality with this lineup, since we were no longer a group of anarchists fueled by activism and revolution who were all on the same page, politically. Warren and I were the only two still sheepishly claiming the title in interviews from time to time. The common denominator among us was a love of getting fucked up. We all liked to party, so we decided to become known as the hardest-partying band.

The more beers we drank, and the more miles we notched on the odometer, the more we started to click and become a tight unit. That first tour together ended in a bonding experience of a drunken game of spin the bottle with a group of college girls in Tennessee. We were all in relationships back in Gainesville, but on that night, it didn't matter. We were willing to tongue-kiss each other for the chance to tongue-kiss them. I made out with Warren, for chrissake. Even thinking about that now makes me feel like there are still beard hairs stuck in my teeth. After the game ended, I left with a tall brunette, and we found an alley doorway to make out in.

"This is probably the worst decision that I've ever made," I told her.

She laughed and smiled, and said, "I'm sure you do this all the time, right?"

I arrived back home filled with guilt over my infidelity. My secret lasted only a couple of hours before coming clean to my wife. She promptly exploded at me in a rage of fists and expletives. I begged for forgiveness, but she raked me over the coals, calling me a child that she had to take care of. Home life turned from miserable to soul-sucking.

We still tried to make it work for a while after that, but Danielle hung it over my head, and became constantly suspicious of me. During one shift at the Top, she found C.C. and me sharing a cigarette in the parking lot and accused us of having an affair. I started becoming suspicious of her, too, hearing rumors around town of guys she was close with. When I read her journal and found out about other men, I moved out, crashing with Andrew and his fiancée, Verité.

Not long after, I was closing down the bar and the Buzzcocks' "Ever Fallen in Love (With Someone You Shouldn't've)" was playing on the jukebox. C.C. pulled me into the handicapped bathroom and locked the door behind us. I thought I was being dragged away to do a quick bump, since that was the best place to do them. Instead she slammed me up against the wall and shoved her tongue down my throat. I pulled her head back by a handful of hair while she bit into my lip with her teeth and tugged at my belt. She pressed against me on the sink, kissing my neck. I felt her breath on my ear as she whispered, "Let's get out of here..."

We left the bar, heading to a hotel on the outskirts of town. I was driving drunk and crashed into a parked car on my way out of the parking lot, but we made it there. The sex was drunken, coked-up, and nervous. I could barely stay hard. I can still picture her after we finished, standing naked in the hotel room, rail-thin, white skin. I counted each rib by the light of passing headlights. I listened to her on the phone, telling her husband that we were finishing up in the bar, that she loved him and she'd be home soon.

I'm sorry. I loved her, too.

"Girl, I'm sorry, but I'm leaving, we're both at fault, we're both to blame. And it wasn't the other men 'cause there were other women. This just isn't love, it's just the remorse of a loss of a feeling. Even if I stayed it just wouldn't be the same."

The success of *Reinventing Axl Rose* garnered the attention of the San Francisco–based independent punk label Fat Wreck Chords, which was owned by NOFX frontman Fat Mike, arguably the world's most famous punk. Despite his penchant for S&M and bestiality humor, Mike is a shrewd businessman, known for his pointy mohawk spikes and blunt attitude.

NOFX had ridden the mid-90s wave of commercially successful punk rock. West Coast bands like them, Green Day, and the Offspring had crossover success into the mainstream, which netted them millions of records sold. Green Day's *Dookie* went diamond after its 1994 release, and the Offspring's *Smash*, with 11 million copies sold, became the best-selling independent release of all time. Not only was Mike prolific with NOFX during this period, but his label reaped the trickle-down rewards of the genre's brief popularity.

We received an email from Toby Jeg, an employee at the label, asking if Against Me! would be interested in recording an EP for Fat's monthly seven-inch club. I turned him down and somewhat brazenly asked if they would instead put out our next full-length. He told me he'd run it by Mike.

James and I were driving when I got the call from Mike, who had done his homework on us. He told us how many copies of *Reinventing* had sold, which was news to us.

"So by my estimation, you guys are worth about $25,000 right now. How about we go with that," he said. "I'll give you $25,000 to put out the next album with Fat Wreck, sound good?"

"Yeah, that sounds reasonable," I said, playing it cool, trying my best not to let my excitement bleed through. Not only was this a guy whose band I grew up listening to, but given that we did our last record for just 800 bucks, $25,000 seemed like all the money in the world.

"How ready are you to record? You almost there?" he asked.

"Totally, we're ready," I said. "The album is written" —which was a total lie. "We can record at the end of the next tour."

We reached an agreement, and I hung up to a raucous celebration. James and I screamed and yelled, hugging each other and punching the van's roof in victory. We were dead fucking broke, and this was more money than any of us had ever seen. We couldn't believe our luck. But not everyone was as excited as we were.

Because Fat Wreck Chords was financially successful, to some in the DIY punk scene, it was considered a "sellout" label, deemed too corporate for punk blood, even though it was technically an indie operation, based out of a downtown office/ warehouse space. Still, we had given No Idea the chance to counteroffer, without telling them we were talking to Fat. We asked for a $2,000 advance to put a down payment on a new van, and they said no. Var, the owner of No Idea, would pay me seven dollars an hour every other week to clean the fish shit out of the tropical fish tanks scattered throughout the office, but he wouldn't help with a tour van. Fat Mike was offering us a comparative fortune. The choice was made.

When word got out that we had "signed" with Fat (even though no paperwork was ever inked, and our arrangement was based entirely on a proverbial handshake), the punks got angry. When I say the punks were angry, I may be understating it a bit. I mean, they were furious. *Maximum Rocknroll*, the zine I'd read religiously as a teenager and used as a guide to book my first tour, published a column in one issue urging people to sabotage our shows at all costs. And they did. People tried to take the instruments out of our hands while we were playing, they threw stink bombs at us on stage, they poured bleach all over our merch, our van became a travelling canvas for their graffiti. For a long time, we drove around with a huge tag on the door, spray-painted by some punks whose outrage was so blindingly strong that it impaired their spelling: AGIANST ME! SUCKS.

After playing a show at a Polish VFW hall on Long Island, New York—a show with an $8 admission that had been set up and promoted by a 16-year-old fan—we drove away in a rumbling van. We pulled over to investigate, only to find that all of our tires had been slashed. During an altercation at another show over our flat tires, some militant DIY punk picked up a brick to threaten us with.

"Go home, you fucking sellout!" he shouted. I turned my back and walked away in disgust. This was the punk scene that meant so much to me? *Fuck this, fuck DIY, and fuck you,* I thought.

Initially I had been attracted to punk and anarchism because I saw them as a means to make a positive change, where everyone was equal. While there were some people in the scene who upheld those values, the more punks I dealt with, the more I realized that most of them were privileged white kids taking advantage of this idealism. On so many occasions, when it came time to divide the door money up at house shows, I witnessed artists get fucked over in the split. I saw what their so-called revolution was really about, and I was over it.

Aside from the small but rabid cabal waged against us, things were going well. Since I had lied to Mike about having a record nearly written, I doubled the working pace on new songs. I frantically penned lyrics in my notebook during downtime on tour, and, in the brief weeks at home, I worked out melodies to accompany them. Miraculously, I cobbled together 12 songs across a summer, and, while most were loud, distorted rock songs, three were stripped-down and acoustic as a nod to Against Me!'s roots.

As promised, Fat Wreck released our second album, *Against Me! as the Eternal Cowboy,* at the end of 2003, and had the resources to actively promote it. All of a sudden, doors were opening for us. We had a publicist and were getting positive press; we had a booking agent and months' worth of touring lined up. The road was wide open in front of us, and we just kept driving. *We're never going home,* I thought to myself.

Our first big tour made us a guaranteed $500 a night opening for Anti-Flag, an established punk band from Pittsburgh. Since they had been professionally touring for years, they ran a tight ship to keep things on schedule. Or at least they tried to. Still having some of that rambunctious teenager in me, for three straight months I bucked against the rules and regulations they imposed, and relentlessly antagonized them. It started on the first day when they handed us our tour laminates, telling us we had to wear them at all times and would be subject to a $20 fee if we lost them. This was so absurd to me that I took my revenge out on them in the form of subtle pranks. When they left Gatorade bottles lying around the green room, I sneaked them out, pissed in them, and put them back. I stole their rider book and hid it until their tour manager had a fit looking for it. I'm not sure if Anti-Flag had assumed they'd be taking us new kids under their wing when they offered us the tour, but I can't imagine they didn't regret the decision to do so.

It felt like we were gaining momentum on the Anti-Flag tour, and fast. We were usually listed in the third slot on a bill of five or six bands, and we blew every other band off the stage every single time, at least in our minds. We picked up more fans each night, and our live show was getting tighter and wilder as people learned our lyrics. When the tour ended, none of us wanted to lose that pace, so we hopped on another one. And another. All in all, we played over 130 shows in 2003 and then over 180 shows in 2004. That's a lot of touring. It was paying off, though, and we built fan bases in every city.

We all loved going to places we had never been before, and jumped at offers to do overseas tours when they started coming in. Now we were slowly crossing all of Europe off the list, and then Australia and Japan, too. I got my first taste of the anarchist scene overseas, and it made me realize how full of shit everyone was back home. The people living in squats in Europe—which were true squats—took care of traveling bands, providing a five-course dinner and beer all night. I was blown away when we arrived in Leipzig, Germany, and entered a huge, run-down concrete building in which the basement club space housed an underground society full of skateboarders riding halfpipes and artists crafting huge sculptures out of metal. These were people truly living off the grid, not just at their moms' houses.

All the travel and excitement around me was distracting and good for my lingering heartbreak over my failed marriage. With no cell phone or internet, I was cut off from the world for months at a time and was starting to feel more at home on the bench seat in the van than in a bed back home.

At age 23, with $13,000 in my bank account, I quit my job checking IDs at the Top. Andrew married Verité; James moved in with his girlfriend, Anne, who was also my roommate; and Warren bought a pool table.

Eternal Cowboy was the start of an era for Against Me!. It was recorded at Ardent Studios in Memphis, Tennessee, a location I chose because I was on a Replacements kick at the time and wanted to do it at the same place they had recorded my favorite album, *Pleased to Meet Me*. I checked the album's liner notes and called the studio listed to book us two weeks there. Upon arriving, I realized it was the nicest studio I'd ever been to, and I felt overwhelmed. Looking at all of the studio's equipment made me nervous about tampering with the raw sound that had come to define Against Me!.

The album solidified the band's musical identity for years to come. After that, Against Me! was officially me, James, Andrew, and Warren. Through writing and recording it, I realized that I would be taking on a new role in the band as its leader. From growing up playing with Kevin, I had always thought music to be a collaborative effort. An ardent anarchist, I believed everyone's efforts to be considered equally. But the guys rarely brought song ideas to practices, so the majority of the songwriting responsibility fell on me. After a while, I stopped trying to force contributions out of them, and I begrudgingly became the group's frontperson.

Not long after *Eternal Cowboy* came out, a strange thing happened. Major labels started taking interest in our little band. I was first contacted by Stay Gold, a sublabel of Universal Records, about putting out our next album. Back then, being juvenile and obnoxiously punk rock as I was, I enjoyed pulling pranks on people. I had seen the Sex Pistols' mockumentary, *The Great Rock 'n' Roll Swindle*, dozens of times. The punk band made hilarity out of embezzling money from big record labels, and I saw this as an opportunity to pull our own version of it.

"There's no way I'm dealing with a *sub*label," I barked at them like a seasoned rock star. "Gimme your boss!" But weirdly enough, not only did Universal not tell me to piss off, they went along with it. A 23-year-old with holes in the bottoms of his sneakers was snapping orders at them through a prepaid cell phone, and they were calling me "Mr. Gabel."

"You'll have to speak to my lawyer about that," I would tell them whenever they called and wanted to talk business. I'd then direct them to Toby from Fat, who acted as our attorney under the name Danny Shapiro, and would "yes" them to death on our behalf.

Other major labels also started reaching out to us about the album, one after another, until it became overwhelming and we needed someone to handle it all. In 2004, when interest in Against Me! was at its highest, we were contacted by Tom Sarig, who at the time managed Le Tigre among other bands, asking if we were looking for management. I held Le Tigre—especially their singer, former Bikini Kill frontwoman and riot grrrl pioneer Kathleen Hanna—in high regard. I thought that if Sarig was a good choice for her band, then he was a good choice for ours, too. Though I'm not sure the rest of the band was sold on him, or on the idea of having a manager in general, I insisted that we have someone representing us, so I hired him. His first order of business was organizing a bidding war among all the major labels—Virgin, Sony, Warner, Universal—and pitting them against each other.

None of this struck me as odd at the time. It seemed like fate being fulfilled. I was young and arrogant, and I felt we deserved the high-profile attention because we were just that good. My politics were flawless, our songs killed, no one was better live than us, I thought. Damn right, major labels should want a piece of us. It was all part of the plan. I had some ego.

Being courted was a sweet feeling, and we milked it for everything it was worth. Label execs would fly us around the country, bring us through their offices, give us stacks of free CDs, and blow tons of smoke up our asses. Their label-speak was something else. They'd compare the four of us to the 1996 Chicago Bulls, which I didn't have the heart to tell them meant nothing to me, since I've never cared about sports.

After years of punk rock asceticism, it was like we had been given the keys to the candy store. They'd buy us drugs, take us out to pricey dinners and strip clubs, and expense everything on the corporate card. We would get lap dances and come over to the A&R people afterward with our hands out. "More. More money, please," we'd tell them, like kids asking for their allowance. We did this until they had to explain that they'd run out of money, at which point we'd get up and leave.

We found the idea of these suits trying to win over a bunch of broke Florida punk kids so absurd and hilarious that we filmed a tour documentary capturing the mockery we made of the experience called *We're Never Going Home*, our very own *Great Rock 'n' Roll Swindle*. We had a friend named Brig from Austin who would always get on stage and cause hilarious, drunken mayhem when we played there, dumping beers on our heads or lifting us up on his shoulders. We flew him out for the tour for the specific purpose of fucking with the label execs whenever they came to our shows. He made sure they were kept neither dry nor comfortable the entire time. For a month, we filmed these poor people being pranked, mocked, and put through hell. Even in the editing, we messed with them, putting flashing dollar signs in their eyes. But I have to give it to them, they hung in there.

Even though it all was a running joke among the band members, it seemed like the numbers we were being sent were going up by the day. Eventually the top bid got up to around $950,000. Meanwhile, Fat Mike had offered us $250,000 to stay with Fat Wreck Chords. After we'd taken this ride as far as we could and there were no more free lap dances to be gotten, the manager told us an answer was needed and whatever our decision was, he would stand behind it.

Something didn't feel right about major labels. The idea of signing to one riddled me with punk guilt. None of us wanted to let money ruin the good thing we had going. All we needed was a van and enough cash to pay rent, anyway. So we unanimously made the decision to stay with Fat for our third album, effectively turning away over half a million dollars.

While I'm sure the major labels were baffled by this from a business standpoint, it felt good to have something in my life I could exert control over. Because with all the action happening around me, deep down, there was something inside that made me feel utterly helpless.

May 18, 2004--Gainesville, FL

    I am completely lost. What voice do
I listen to? What urge do I follow? I
woke up this morning and turned on the
TV to a Learning Channel documentary on

transgender people. The documentary talked
about how one in 30,000 has the "disorder."
They dissected brains, they found results.

Wide awake now at 4:15 AM. As I sober
up, my mind fixates on the same hopelessness that it always does. I feel anger
towards everyone and everything. I seethe
venom. All I can see is a hard landing
after a fall. My soul is drifting. Gainesville stays the same.

How many years am I going to spend
staring at dresses in store windows wishing
they were mine? I pray for something or
someone to save me.

———————

June 11, 2004--Milan, Italy

The band and crew were all hungry after
the show tonight. The promoter took us to
a roadside food truck. As we were order-
ing, three gorgeous women came walking up.
There was the tall leggy blonde in blue
jeans and a white tube top over a leopard print bra. There was the short brunette with glasses, a sequined backless
top and matching mini-skirt. There was the
gaunt brunette with a ponytail wearing a
tight white tank top with a Playboy bunny
printed on it and a super tiny pleated
black mini-skirt.

"Holy shit!" said Andrew under his breath before beginning to laugh.

When I looked again, I realized that the three women were transsexuals. I saw they had no hips and that the brunette with her hair down was balding. I heard their voices as they ordered food. Their tits were real though.

We all gawked and joked amongst ourselves, not very discreetly at all. Regardless of whether or not they spoke English, they knew that we were talking about them. Our roadie Black Arm John was so freaked out, he went and stood on the other side of the road until we were ready to go.

"I think the brunette in the black skirt is actually a girl."

"Why don't you suck her dick and find out?"

"You guys want to get a brostitute?"

"Prostidudes!"

I laughed at them along with everyone else, the whole time knowing the truth about myself, that I wished I were so brave.

Not knowing who you are is a terrible feeling.

I've been called a "sellout" many times in life for the choices I've made in my musical career. But this experience, that moment--that's what it feels like to truly sell out.

June 26, 2004--Rechlin-Lärz Airfield

I was in a bad mood as we headed to the
festival show but I couldn't have been more
wrong about how the night was going to go.
It was exactly what we all needed to push
us through the last couple days of this
tour.

The Fusion Festival was held on the
Rechlin-Lärz Airfield, a now-abandoned air
base where German jet fighters once took
flight from. Our set was before Nomeansno,
who were then followed by Chumbawamba. So
amazing to have the chance to see Chumbawamba play despite the fact that their
set was plagued with technical difficul-
ties. They are one of my favorite bands.

I bought six hits of ecstasy off my
friend Gunnar and passed each one out to
everyone in the band and crew, saying that
we all had to take them, and making sure
everyone knew that under no circumstances
could we let Martin "the Metal Angel" know
we were high on ecstasy because while Martin was fine with drinking and smoking
weed, he was absolutely NOT cool with a
considerably harder drug like MDMA.

Neither Andrew, Jordan, nor John had
ever taken ecstasy before. We dosed while
still wet with stage sweat. After packing up our gear, we headed out onto the

festival grounds to watch bands. James
and I got somehow separated from everyone in the crowds of people. An hour
passes and we start to get worried that
I'd been ripped off with fake drugs but
then the pill kicks in with a vengeance. Everything became absolutely fucking
hilarious, the two of us laughing wildly,
wandering around the festival while looking for the rest of the gang.

We eventually found Jordan, Warren, and
John, but still no Andrew. All of a sudden, Andrew comes flying through the
crowd, pupils the size of dinner plates,
covered head to toe in some kind of white
powder yelling wildly about the new group
of German friends he's made and how we
should all relocate to Germany.

Flash Gordon was playing on large movie
screens. Raves of people dancing, fire
shooting into the sky, the beat thump-
ing in your chest. We were all fuuuuuu-
ucked uuuuuuup. Everything was so right.
Everything made sense in the world. I
didn't want to ever come down. I wanted to
stay that high, stay that young and free
forever.

We didn't head back to the hostel until
after the sun was up. It was just time
to go. I had smoked four final joints,
drank two whole bottles of champagne, and
just couldn't get any more fucked up. I

switched through songs on the van's stereo,
anxiously looking for the right one to
compliment the moment, eventually landing
on the Leatherface song "Plastic Surgery."
A perfect moment. The best of times with
my best of friends.

When the band's success couldn't keep the dysphoria at bay, I relied on cocaine and sex to do the trick. I was fucking C.C., I was fucking the booking agent, I was still fucking my estranged wife, I was fucking anyone who would fuck me back. Then it all caught up with me at once.

I was supposed to get on a plane and fly west to California for a high-profile magazine photo shoot, but had stayed awake all night getting high. I was not a great flyer, and the feeling of dread at the thought of getting on a plane grew stronger and stronger with each line I snorted and each hour that passed.

By sunrise, I had convinced myself that the plane was going to crash. But I knew I couldn't talk my way out of the obligation, so I skipped town, turned off my cell phone, and didn't tell anyone where I was going. I drove to Cedar Key, a fishing village on the Gulf Coast just west of Gainesville. I checked into a motel, walked to the closest bar, and sat down for a drink.

Tacked to the wall across from where I sat at the bar was a newspaper article detailing the 1977 plane crash deaths of Ronnie Van Zant, Steve Gaines, and Cassie Gaines of Lynyrd Skynyrd. I interpreted this as cosmic affirmation that my premonition had indeed been correct and that had I gotten on that plane, it would have most assuredly gone down.

Drunk and alone, lying in the dark of my hotel room later

that night, I reached into my pants to jerk off and stopped after feeling something out of the ordinary. I turned on the light to find bumps covering my legs and groin.

My mind immediately jumped to the conclusion that it was some horrible STD and that God was punishing me. In my cocaine-fueled paranoia, I convinced myself that I had contracted HIV. I began to prepare for death.

I soon started attending Narcotics Anonymous meetings in secret. I became diligent about making doctor appointments to have my blood screened for disease, although none was ever found. I was sure they were all lying.

I had been reckless in my sexual endeavors, sleeping with strangers or with women I knew to be loose, sleeping with an intravenous drug user, never using proper protection. I was out of control, and this was a reality check. As part of the forgiveness stage of my Narcotics Anonymous redemptive process, I contacted my most recent sexual partners to apologize for what an asshole I'd been. I told them about the infection and asked if they'd also experienced any symptoms, but none had.

September 26, 2004--Gainesville, FL

The last person I had sex with was C.C. We were both drunk. That was almost a year ago. I haven't been with anyone since.

That first time in the examination room, waiting for a doctor to come say what's wrong with me, I swore off all vices, no more sex, no more drinking, no more drugs, no more pornography, eat all my vegetables, anything, God, please. Please just make this go away.

A week later the test results come back
and I'm told that I don't have Hepatitis. I
don't have Syphilis. I don't have herpes.
There's something in my head that won't
let me believe though. None of them can
see the real disease.

I go to another clinic and I'm tested
for Chlamydia and Gonorrhea.

A young blonde nurse tells me that just
by looking at my cock she can see that I
don't have either of the diseases.

"There's no discharge," she says.

I ask her to test anyway. She obliges
by shoving a wooden Q-tip into my
dickhole.

For a second I think I feel empathy
coming from her, which endears her to me.
Fate has linked us. There is a bond. We
will always have shared this moment, an
STD test, a Q-tip, my dick in your hands.
I almost ask her out on a date.

She tells me to make an appointment
with a dermatologist. The bruising on the
inside of my leg keeps growing. I'm thinking they're going to have to amputate
my leg. It looks like there's a parasite
inside of me eating away.

I spend night after night sitting
naked on my bathroom floor in total
self-disgust. The dermatologist prescribed
a steroid cream for the bruising.

I go to another walk-in clinic, and am
able to talk the doctor into giving me a

full physical, a tetanus shot, the first
of three shots for Hepatitis B, just in
case.

I also get blood drawn for HIV testing
again.

This is the fourth time I've been tested
in the last six weeks.

Results always come back in the clear,
the doctor always tells me that there's
nothing wrong with me, that it's all in my
head.

"What about this line on my cock?" I
ask while quickly taking my dick out of my
pants to turn over and show him. I speak
as if I'm talking with a mechanic about
something being wrong with my car.

"I wouldn't be worried about that if I
were you," he diagnoses.

"What about the molluscum?"

"There's nothing you can do about it.
The sooner you get healthy, the sooner it
will go away. I tell you that every time,
Tom. Quit using drugs. Get clean."

Though my neuroses got the best of me, in reality, I'd find
out that my condition was not sexually transmitted at all. It was
molluscum contagiosum, a viral bacterial skin infection common among children. Years of living in filth and wearing clothes
out of dumpsters had finally caught up to me. I was so fucked
up on drugs and alcohol that my immune system wasn't able to
fight it.

On tour, I had been crashing in dingy, mice-infested European squats and wearing sweaty show pants for months at a time,

going weeks without taking a shower. I'd already dealt with scabies multiple times, as well as impetigo, but I didn't see the connection. I obsessed over my condition. Both the paranoia and physical symptoms only worsened with constant substance abuse.

While I was really just in desperate need of a long, salicylic acid bath, more than anything, my soul felt dirty. I wasn't getting drunk or high for fun or escape anymore; it was out of habit and dependency. It suddenly hit me that I was not simply a casual user of drugs and alcohol; I was a full-on addict. I was closing out the Top every night, drowning myself in gin and tonics, two grams of coke, half a pack of cigarettes, and the occasional bag of mushrooms. This was my daily routine.

The innocence of youth was gone, replaced by something more sinful and perverse. All the noise around me about what it meant to sell out, all the people asking for something from me or telling me they wanted to do something for me, all the chaos and confusion in the face of mortality. It was overwhelming. I wanted that sense of clarity back. I wanted to be healthy again. This psychosis, fueled by dysphoria, addiction, and disease, became the inspiration for the songs I would write for our third album, *Searching for a Former Clarity*.

August 21, 2004--Arizona

Our hotel room smells like kitty litter and costs too much money.
Was offered some blow after the show tonight. A cold sweat washed over my body. My mouth started to salivate. I could already taste it running down the back of my throat before the dollar bill was even rolled.

How much is too much?

I lay awake in bed past sunrise, praying that my heart doesn't explode.

Line after line after line.

I do a line off the toilet before I take a shower. I do a line before I take a pill. I do a line before I get in bed. I do a line before I do another line until I'm dead.

If it weren't for pills and alcohol I would never sleep.

This fucking rotten disease, it's not going away unless I get healthy. Six days ago my face started breaking out. Molluscum bumps around my temples, across my forehead, and on my nose.

I've started carrying a bottle of hand sanitizer in my pocket. Regularly taking a multi-vitamin and a vitamin E supplement. I've been changing my boxer shorts at least twice a day. I look at myself and see a drug addict, alcoholic, STD-ridden, self-obsessed asshole.

I want to be so much more than this. For two nights in a row now I've fantasized about a waitress who served me coffee in Bend, OR. Something about her beauty has stuck with me for days. I wish I was her.

It doesn't look like it feels on the inside.

September 11, 2004--Sydney, Australia

Two sold-out shows back to back at the
Annandale Hotel. Tonight was the best of
the two. Blinding white light everywhere,
sweat dripping, my eardrums all but bleeding. Every move ballet. The experience was
reason for which I still have faith. We
celebrate by drinking all night at the bar.

"I bet her mouth is really warm," says
James; and then he quickly slaps a hand
over his mouth.

The bartenders fucking hate us. We are
anything but discreet as we gawk at their
tits and asses. A bunch of dudes being
dudes, practically jerking themselves off
in public.

This is a tough front to wear.

I lick the salt off my hand, down the
shot and bite into the lemon. I feel my
stomach turn. I know I'm about to throw
up. I race to the bathroom. I make it to
the toilet just barely before throwing up
five times. Pieces of half-digested salad
and kebab fill my nose and then get sucked
back down into my throat as I gasp for air.

———

November 20, 2004--Somewhere in Virginia

Cocaine-fueled insomnia.
Sudden mood swings and depression.

Binge drinking, binge eating, binge masturbation.

Is this any way to live?

I pretend to feel because I'm so tired of feeling nothing.

Who am I if I am not who I pretend to be?

If I were to say how I really feel,

What I really think,

People would think I was mentally ill.

Cross-dressing feels like self-mutilation.

I can never be anything more than a pervert dressed up in women's clothes.

So sick, sick, sick.

I want to black it all out.

I do not care if I am alive or dead.

It takes time to decompress after coming home from a tour. You feel like your body is still moving. You grow to crave the constant stimulation that comes from being on the road, always going to a new place every day, meeting new people, having new experiences. You have a purpose each day: to play a show. Good or bad, it's a daily accomplishment. I would return home from tour and instantly realize how alone and aimless I was.

Being locked in a van with the same people for 100 hours a week makes you feel like you're living in your own little world. Subjects that comprise your daily conversations become so weird and esoteric that to outsiders, you have nothing of relatable interest to say. All of your jokes are inside jokes, all of your stories are about the road. I was quickly growing disconnected with friends in the Gainesville scene. Gainesville is small and gossipy, and all the rampant cocaine use made me paranoid about everything—major label attention and the fallout from punks, convinced I was dying of undiagnosed diseases, believing I was schizophrenic and losing my mind, lost in dysphoria.

I was physically and mentally run down from the road, two years of straight touring, two years of drinking and drugging. I still wasn't legally divorced, and thought that maybe giving closure to the relationship would change the way I felt inside my head; that maybe sobering up and changing my ways would give me a feeling of redemption for all my sins, real or imagined.

When I couldn't maintain control of my personal life, I overcompensated by micromanaging the band, insisting that we practice six nights a week. My authoritarian leadership was putting a strain on us, and I could sense the rest of the band turning on me. What started out as a fun excuse to travel the world and party was starting to feel more like a job. Expectations were weighing on us, and I didn't want to let down the people depending on us—the fans, the label, the manager.

For Christmas, the manager sent me a brand new Blackberry as a gift. I'm sure his motivation was to keep tabs on me so that I wasn't unreachable for weeks at a time on tour when he needed a quick answer on something. But when the rest of the band received fruit baskets, it sent a clear message that I somehow mattered more than anyone else, which drove a wedge further between us. I could sense that they all resented the manager, or maybe they just resented me for hiring him. James is the kind of person who can go a whole conversation without saying more than two words, but those two words will be really funny and capture it all: Dumbfounded upon receiving his fruit basket, he joked: "Well, I guess mediocrity gets you pears." If nothing else, it inspired a song title.

Just before Christmas, I went to visit my father in Missouri. By that point, it felt like we were just going through the motions in our relationship. We had grown more and more distant over the years as he settled into his new life with his second wife. She came from a large family and their house was covered in photos of them, but the only photos of me and Mark were a couple tucked away in my dad's office. My brother didn't even come that Christmas. Recently he'd had a falling-out with my father after calling him out on not wanting to spend time with us. To her credit, though, our stepmom also grew up on hair metal, drove a T-top Firebird Trans Am, smoked Capri cigarettes, and had a killer collection of 80s band T-shirts. She gifted me a Led Zeppelin box set, and I still love the band because of her.

My dad hated all the tattoos I'd accumulated over the years and didn't seem to take my career as a musician seriously. It seemed like all we'd talk about were things he disapproved of. Knowing the forced, awkward holiday conversations that awaited me, I took my time getting there, making the drive from Florida in over a week. On the way, I stayed at inconspicuous Nowheresville motels throughout the South, drinking and becoming her.

December 25, 2004--Naples, FL

Drunk on Christmas, missing my soon to be ex-wife while also wishing that we had never met and that our whole relationship never happened. What could anyone possibly see in me when I'm so full of self-hatred?

I can't meet anyone new until I get
healthy.

Drunk on Christmas, feeling burnt out
from a long year on the road, thinking
back through all the shows, a blur of
stages, dressing rooms, and hotel rooms.
More names and faces than I can ever possibly hope to remember.

I want something to take away this horrible frantic feeling inside of me.

I see the older punks around Gainesville, night after night, year after year,
holding down that same seat at the bar.
They'll never leave this place, never grow
out of drinking tall cans in a swamp.
This may be enough for them but it's not
enough for me.

I want punk rock to still mean
something.

I'm not really taking any chances with
my art.

Will I ever be anything more than a boy
dressed up in women's clothes?

I always make a New Year's resolution, so in the days leading
to December 31, 2004, I made the decision to sober up while
starting work on a third album. I got better, and the skin infection
gradually cleared up, but I became a wound-up ball of stress, not
a very fun person to be around. I was what you might call a prick.

I also committed myself to being male; no more cross-dressing.
It wasn't doing me any good to perpetuate an impossible fantasy,
although this habit was a bit harder to break. A bag hidden in the

back of my closet contained my collection of women's underwear from Walmart and Target. It wasn't until the end of February that I worked up the nerve to sneak it out of the house. I sealed everything up in a garbage bag and tossed it into a supermarket dumpster.

On New Year's Eve, I went on one last gender-bender before sobering up the next morning as I'd promised myself.

January 1, 2005--Gainesville, FL

I run into this girl I know at a party and the next thing I know, we're lying on the floor of my furniture-less house, passionately making out. A friend is passed out beside us. We're drunk on gin and tonics and high on cocaine. I close my eyes and pretend that she is someone I love, that she is someone who loves me. I run my fingers through her hair and trace the outline of her face. I don't remember falling asleep and we wake up in each other's arms, awkward and hung over. I tell her that I'll call her but I won't.

I know what will happen if I keep getting high. I've been getting high since I was 13 years old. What I don't know is what will happen if I can stay sober. Eventually, life has to change. That change may come violently and suddenly, but it will come...right?

My New Year's resolution for 2005 is to be sober.

January 13, 2005--Gainesville, FL

The divorce is final. I am no longer
married.

Last night, after the courthouse,
I went out to Paynes Prairie with my
ex-wife. We brought all of the letters we
had ever written to each other as well as
small gifts we had exchanged and buried
them in the ground. We carved our initials into the closest fence post, like a
gravestone marker for our marriage. Once
the ceremony was finished, we stood up and
walked the path back to the road together,
got on our bikes, and rode off on our
separate ways.

The feeling of closure is unsettling. A
part of my heart had turned rotten. For
the past three years, it had been pumping
nothing but hate, spite, and nihilism. And
this morning when I woke up, it was gone.

January 28, 2005--Naples, FL

Dad called today. I mentioned how we're
buying a new van and that we're paying
cash. I immediately worry that I sound
like I'm boasting. I'm just talking to fill
the silence.

Sometimes when I see that it's my dad calling, I imagine that it's actually my stepmother calling to say that he has died.

I bought a 27" TV for $200 from Walmart and a $20 couch from the Salvation Army. I have anxiety over buying things. I'm not used to having money.

We demoed twelve songs in eight hours at Goldentone Studio here in town. As the engineer and owner, Rob, was mixing, we all got really excited about what we were hearing and started talking about how we should save a bunch of money and just record here in Gainesville at Goldentone. Fat Mike called coincidentally and I couldn't contain the excitement. I told him our idea and he really got behind it. He said this is what he's thought we should do all along. By the time we leave the studio, we've decided to record the album next week and ditch the plan of looking for a producer to work with. We also agree to fire the manager at some point. We all hate the manager.

It takes about as long as the van ride home from the studio for the excitement over our big plan to start wearing off. Self-doubt creeps in. Fat Mike calls back in the morning and says having thought about it more, we should probably keep looking for a producer as planned. We all turn back on our decision to fire the manager too. No one is brave enough to fully commit.

As we're unloading equipment from the van, I start to sense a tension among us. I call off practice for the next couple of days and start driving south.

I haven't had a drink in 28 days.

———————

February 17, 2005--Gainesville, FL

The folk singer stands up on a chair in the middle of the Wayward Council non-profit volunteer-run record store to announce the start of his set. He slowly strums his guitar and sings while throwing in jokes between verses. He jumps off the chair and is standing in the center of the room by the end of the song. He makes everyone sing along to the lyrics, "The greatest thing in the world is to love someone and for them to love you back." It was a beautiful thing to witness and to be a part of.

Before he starts to play his next song, he goes on a diatribe. "This is our space, this is real. Fuck stages and division between band and audience. Fuck rock stars and bands with bumper stickers, websites, and $12 ticket prices."

I am immediately alienated and no longer feel welcome in the room. Where are you supposed to go when you no longer feel welcome in the places you turned to because you didn't feel welcome anywhere else?

February 18, 2005—Gainesville, FL

There is a bag in my closet containing two blonde wigs and women's clothing. I'm not sure I look good as a blonde. I live alone but still I keep the bag pushed shamefully to the very back of my closet, hidden behind a stack of shoeboxes. It would shatter me if someone discovered my secret.

I get this urge, all these inescapable thoughts come at me. Nothing but feeding the urge gives me calm. I guess you could call them "episodes." At the end, when it's time to undress and stop pretending, after I've acted on the impulse, I just feel fucked up.

My earliest memories are of dressing up in my mother's clothes and I am constantly reduced by the shame I feel in remembering. Five years old in a fort made of sheets, blankets, and chairs, enamored with the feeling of my legs in pantyhose. I was not taught nor did I learn the behavior by example; it came to me naturally. It's part of me.

I think my problems with drug use and
alcoholism can be directly attributed to
living with the shame I have over these
feelings.

By mid-April, we were ready to record *Searching for a Former Clarity*. So far I had kept my resolution to stay sober. I had become obsessive-compulsive about my health following my infection. In addition to my regular doctor visits, Andrew and I started spending two hours at the gym every morning, five days a week.

I cherished this extracurricular bonding time to lift weights with Andrew. I wanted to be his best friend, but he seemed to have reservations about it. Whenever he referred to a particular buddy back home as his "best friend," it hurt my feelings a bit. Andrew makes friends easily, and I've always struggled with that. He's a real "man's man," which made me feel inferior; as if people could see the truth about me in comparison. Although I knew I could never be someone like that, it was the disguise I wanted—to be like all the other dudes.

We checked in to the Carlyle Apartments in Baltimore, Maryland, which would be our home for the next month while we recorded at Magpie Cage there, and then mixed at Inner Ear in DC before heading off to tour.

We didn't know what a producer did exactly, but we had either convinced ourselves or been talked into believing that we needed one. Either way, it was going to be an experience outside of our comfort zone that would make us learn something, and I knew that I wanted that. So after much internal deliberation, and at Warren's suggestion, we chose to work with J. Robbins.

J. had produced albums by bands like the Promise Ring, Jets

to Brazil, and Clutch, and had played bass in the DC hardcore band Government Issue. I loved the Jets to Brazil records, musically and sonically, and the scene he came from was the complete polar opposite of Fat Wreck Chords. These were respected, influential rock bands, not the goofy, board short–wearing pop punk bands we'd been relegated to. I was sold.

Five weeks were scheduled to record and mix. Our first album had been recorded and mixed in two days. The second, two weeks. We didn't know what we would do with all this studio time.

J. had a calm and laid-back demeanor. We all liked him immediately. Our work schedule was 11 AM to 11 PM, Monday through Saturday. The studio had no windows and a collection of equipment nicer than anything any of us owned. J.'s dog, Doctor Robert, sat at his feet or on his lap while we tracked. Although the setup was very professional, I've never been convinced J. actually liked any of the songs we recorded with him.

April 20, 2005--Baltimore, MD

We tracked drums for "Miami," "The Energizer," "Problems," "Sex," "The Roller," and "How Low" today, spending the most time on "Miami."

Everyone was tense as usual when we first start playing in the morning. Warren's tempos are all over the place, no consistency. I don't know what to say to calm everyone down so I say nothing and play on.

J. suggests Warren plays along to a click track, which he thankfully agrees to do, but even with the click, J. still

had to do a lot of editing to get steady
drum takes. This is the first time we've
recorded with Pro Tools and we're leaning
heavily on it. This is also the first time
we've worked with a real producer, or better put, really been produced.

My impulse is do everything as in-the-
moment as possible, that's the punk ethos.
It's about the spirit, not the technical
ability, but I can't argue with the results
I'm hearing. I want the album to sound
good. I want the playing to be in tune
and on time. The four of us all spend
so much time playing in this band, why
wouldn't we want it to sound tight? This
album will definitely have a more produced
sound than we've ever had before, but
that's what I want, isn't it?

When J. tells Andrew that he reminds
him of a friend who is "one of the
greats," all I hear him saying is that
I am not one of the greats. How am I considered? My general suspicion is that most
people find me peculiar, anxious, egotistical, arrogant, with big ears.

April 23, 2005--Baltimore, MD

No coffee or diet Cokes today, just tea
with lemon. Horrible mood. I tried singing tonight and nothing came out. My throat

is fucked. J. could tell how frustrated and
discouraged I was. We called it a day early,
he told us all we should go back to the
hotel and relax, get a good night's sleep.
He also recommended I go to a walk-in
clinic and try to get a shot of cortisone
to help get me through tracking vocals. The
doctor wouldn't give me the shot and instead
wrote me a prescription for Amoxicillin.

Stressing out about not being able to
sing is only making my voice worse. Take a
breath. You can get through this.

There's a book in the studio about snow-
boarding, skateboarding, and music, with
a quote from a snowboarder stating his
view on making a living. "If you go out
there and do it, give it all that you've
got, then you're already a pro. But if you'd
walk away from it once the money stops,
then you're just a jock."

Tonight at dinner the desire for just
a glass of wine was strong. Drunk, sober,
who cares? I'm still an asshole.

I'm going to visit Edgar Allan Poe's grave
tomorrow. Good place to go and think.

———————

May 4, 2005--Baltimore, MD

Our last full day of tracking.
I wince at every word while we listen
to the playback of the last song on the

album, "Searching for a Former Clarity."
God only knows what everyone in the room
is thinking. Or are they thinking anything
at all? The song ends and I can breathe
again. The album is finished. There it is,
we all just heard it.

We are all sitting in the control room
sharing some laughs and a small moment of
triumph. J. asks if we have a name for the
album. I still hadn't said anything to the
rest of the band.

"I want to call the album *Searching for
a Former Clarity.*"

Nothing. The mood in the room quickly
turns to disappointment. The silence is
uncomfortable. No one says anything in
response, not a single word. J. quickly
diverts the conversation elsewhere.

I'm trying not to care if anyone else
likes it but feeling pessimistic. These
songs are crap. I am an insignificant,
pathetic fool.

When record labels fight each other to offer you nearly
a million dollars, and you turn them all down, you might
assume that this would be a pretty clear bridge-burning with
the music industry. But oddly enough, after Fat Wreck Chords
released *Searching for a Former Clarity* in the fall of 2005,
the major label interest came back—and it came back stronger
than ever.

It was ironic that Against Me! was still heavily on the music industry's radar, given how hard I'd railed against it all throughout *Searching*, with lyrics like "We'll give the money back to the record label / Fire the agent, fire the manager / We ain't got what it takes to make it / We got indifference, got no respect for them." But labels weren't actually listening to the music; they were more focused on the album's hype. It was our first record to crack the Billboard 200, and it was reviewed in *Rolling Stone*. So the whole major label courting process started all over again. Another round of dinners and drinks on the corporate card, another round of lap dances, another round of smoke up our asses.

Fat Mike, on the other hand, thought the album was shit. He told me that he hated J.'s production style, didn't like the mix or the track listing, and that the cover art (a black and white photo of a Florida palm tree) was terrible. "Make the band name bigger!" This took the wind out of our sails a bit and started making me consider our next move.

The reason we had stayed indie, signed no contract, and taken less money was for artistic freedom. But now we found ourselves with no contract, in a punk rock handshake deal, but still compromising and fighting with our label over things like artwork and songs.

A punk band signing to a major label has historically been a risky endeavor, one that has crushed bands under its pressure. The story of Jawbreaker is infamous in the punk scene. The band got a million dollars to release their fourth album, *Dear You*, in 1995, but the backlash from fans was so great and the sales were so dismal that the band broke up shortly after. Numerous other bands have similar war stories of being torn apart by the high expectations of the corporate world.

To me, it was a gamble either way. The chances that we would ever break into the mainstream were just as good as the chances that we would implode from the stagnation of for-ever staying a Fat Wreck Chords band. Our expiration date was always there in the back of my mind. While the rest of the band might've enjoyed the steady paycheck, I don't think they saw Against Me! as a long-term investment—especially Warren, who from time to time offhandedly mentioned that he was considering becoming a history teacher, completely disregarding the education and training he'd need for a career like that. If we didn't keep evolving—even if that evolution drew detractors—we would surely grow stale, and the interest in Against Me! would die down, from both the fans and internally. I'd rather risk it all and go out with a bang than fade into obscurity.

The potential for Against Me!'s growth had personal implications for me, as well. In my newfound sobriety, I could no longer chase away my dysphoria by throwing drugs and alcohol at it, so I thought I could kill it with fame. Maybe if we were the biggest band in the world—if we played stadiums and sold millions of records, if we had legions of fans and hit singles on the radio—all of the urges and the cross-dressing would go away. I told our booking agent that we wanted the works: a 50-state tour to end the year. Do whatever it took to keep us on the road, so I could outrun my shame.

Our largest-ever tour kicked off with our largest-ever shows, three nights opening for Green Day in massive arenas, all while the majors chased after us again. In the same week that we launched into our three-month conquest of the entire country, we made our network television debut, performing *Searching for a Former Clarity*'s single, "Don't Lose Touch," on *Late Night with Conan O'Brien*. I called my parents and told them to tune in to watch me on national television. It was real, tangible success I could finally point them to. Even my father seemed impressed in his own stoic way.

August 11, 2005--NYC--The Chelsea Hotel

We were fighting jet lag and never
really found our rhythm tonight but now
we can say we played the legendary CBGBs.
When loading in, the owner, Hilly Kristal,
was just sitting there at his desk with his
feet propped up, no hello, no thanks for
playing, nothing. We're playing for free.
It's a benefit show for his closing club.
I'm glad this club is closing. It deserves
to close down. Fuck this place and whatever
happened here back in the day. It's not
special. Every place and everything eventually needs to end. The spirit of whatever
happened here is long gone, this is just a
tourist attraction now.

Felt like we were going through the
motions on stage. Our set reeked of
predictability. There we are on stage
exhausted, making the safe choices, playing the safe songs in the safe order. The
150 kids who bought tickets are up front
singing along. The 150 guest listed industry types are in the back watching and
judging. I'm wondering afterwards what
they really think of the show. Did they
really like it? Or are they just interested because they think that other people
are? I have a feeling that if the fans,
the people who really get it, stopped coming out then the businessmen wouldn't be
so interested anymore.

Vanessa, our publicist, brought me a
copy of the new album to the hotel after
the show. Here I am, holding it in my
hands. I don't know what to feel. Do I
like the way it looks? I don't know. I'm
not even sure what it sounds like anymore. A full year's worth of work, all the
stress and worry summed up in the compact
disc I'm holding here.

—————

September 2, 2005--Driving to Massachusetts

Flying into Newark we passed directly
over Giants Stadium. I looked down and
could see the stage we'll be playing the
next day. From up above, it all looked so
small. There will be over 50,000 people
in attendance at tomorrow's show where
we're opening up for Green Day. I have no
idea what to expect. It's hard to imagine what a crowd of 50,000 people looks
like.

I wasn't nervous when we took the stage.
There had been a lot of build-up leading to the day, but I knew we were just
the opening band and we were prepared, we
knew what we were doing. As long as we had
fun, I knew it would be good.

Family and friends, old and new came,
out to the show, as did the manager and
A&R from Universal. All of them stood on

the side of the stage to show support and
cheer us on.

Looking over my shoulder and seeing everyone there, I felt love and I appreciated
it. It hurts in my chest and it's wonder-
ful. It meant a lot that Dustin made it to
the show. I only wished that he was still
playing with the band.

Even the guys from Green Day watched
the set. Green Day was the first concert
I ever went to. It was a personal achievement to share a stage with them and I'll
be forever thankful for the experience. A
great big "fuck you" to every asshole cop
and teacher who tried to tell me I was
nothing, just a punk.

If I remember anything about yesterday,
I want it to be that feeling of love. We'll
never return to Giants Stadium as a headliner, they'll tear it down before we ever
have the chance.

The analogy that A&R from Universal
Records used tonight is my favorite I've
heard come out of his mouth thus far.

"Pretend you're going to be in a motor-
cycle race. Conor Oberst has a bike, Moby
has his. Now, it doesn't matter what you
put in your bike, it could be the best
fuel ever. The bike will only go as fast
as it was built to go, and right now,
boys...we're putting rocket fuel in a
moped."

He really knows how to sell. He doesn't
really have to try so hard though. I want
what he's selling.

———————

September 6, 2005--West Palm Beach, FL

Our album has been officially released.
No one in the band says anything about it.
The moment is unfulfilling. I don't think
I'll ever be able to get what I need emotionally from this band. I'm trying to put
on a smile and be positive but it makes me
feel like a liar, which makes me want to
drink.
    Here I am, nine months sober. Has any-
thing changed? Do I feel any better for it?
    Right now I just feel crushed.
    I woke up last night and my left arm
was completely numb and lifeless. I took
a shower. I started thinking about Mary
the Baptist being abused by her preacher.
I came close to jerking off but I stopped
myself. I turned off the shower and got
out, restrained myself from punching a hole
in the cheap plastic shower wall. Ejacu-
lated in my sleep last night. It's been nine
months since I last masturbated. I'm a big
ball of stress, tension, and bad feelings.
    I'd rather live an exciting life drunk
than a boring life sober.

September 15, 2005--NYC--12:08 AM

Today I met with David Johansen of the
New York Dolls, a band that pioneered the
idea of blurring gender lines of rock
and roll in the 70s. We met at a tea shop
around the corner from the Road Runner
offices. He wants me to help write for his
new album. I had the chills and was sweating profusely. My brain was saturated in
NyQuil. I'm positive that my awkwardness
was apparent to everyone.

David is super skinny, with leath-
ery skin, and long greasy hair. His bangs
cover his eyes. I asked the questions I
had thought to ask but as I was asking
them I realized how stupid they were.

"What kind of album do you all want to
make?"

David asks me how old I am and I felt
my youth and inexperience.

He gave me his number and said we
should just start bouncing ideas off of
each other. He said he likes me. I'm not
sure I believe him.

There's a *Fader* after-party in the evening that the manager insists we all go to.
Even though I'm sick, I go anyways. I made
it through unscathed. I actually had fun.

The press around our new album is good.
More than good, really. The major label

interest is back with a vengeance. All of
the attention we're getting is enjoyable.
I like being a buzz band. I like being
courted by A&R men and record labels.

Universal A&R was at the *Fader* party.
"Do you ever just realize how good you
are?" he asks.

My ass is full of smoke.

———

September 18, 2005--New Haven, CT--1:34 AM

The manager emailed to let us know that
we're #1 at commercial specialty radio this
week.

It's the first show of a three-month
long 50-state tour. It wasn't until the
first opening band was playing that I
started to feel the excitement, it's all
really happening. My voice is already
shredded. My throat feels caked with
crust. It hurts to sing. This is going to
be a long tour, draining both mentally and
physically, but what an opportunity.

We're in the middle of the set and
I'm on my knees in front of my amp,
sweat pouring from my body, fighting to
breathe. I am living fully and completely.
There's no rush, no hurry, there is no
place else I'd rather be, surrounded by
strangers, bodies pressed tightly together,
amidst deafening noise and blinding

confusion all is silent and completely at
peace.

――――――――

October 1, 2005--Milwaukee, WI--The Rave--
3:12 AM

   I'm hungover, my first hangover in nine
full months. I've been sleeping off last
night in the back of the van all day.
I'm disappointed in myself. I broke my
resolution. I didn't make it the full year.
I'm scared that I've ruined something, that
by having a drink I destroyed some kind of
magic.
   After the show at Rhino's in Bloomington, Indiana, we all headed over to a bar
across the street to watch our performance
on *Conan*. During the commercial break,
right before our performance, shots were
poured and a toast was made. I broke down.
I wanted to share in the moment with everyone. Andrew did a quick toast and we
watched ourselves perform on national TV.
Just one shot. Six shots and a couple of
beers later I'm sitting at the bar next to
the bass player of the opening band and
we're both groping each other under the
table. Next thing I know we're standing in
the parking lot making out. She tells me
she has a boyfriend in California. Fuck.
Then black out.

The *Rolling Stone* review compares my
voice to Roger Daltrey's. They gave the
album 3 out of 5 stars and cited "How Low"
as the key track.

————————

October 14, 2005--Seattle, WA--4:15 AM

I thought I was having a heart attack.
Two overnight drives, Salt Lake City to
Boise, Boise to Seattle. We're broken up
into rentals, two mini-vans and a box
truck for gear and merch. The oil pump
broke again on the Ford. No sleep. I think
I must have had ten Red Bulls over the
course of the two drives. Grew so crazed
at one point, pulled over, and Black Arm
John and I built a snowman while everyone
slept. We named him Skinny and are just
sure we'll see him again down the line.
No time to rest once we got to Seattle.
Too many friends to see. Last night was
the 27th show in a row that we've played
on this tour. Not a single day off. Sold
out show at Neumos, get up on stage feeling dizzy. I can't even get a chord out
of my guitar when the band kicks in, I
can't open my lungs to sing. My chest was
unbearably tight with pain. Whole left
side went numb. I stood there and did what
I could, got us to the end of the set. The
audience could tell something wasn't right

though. What should have been a riot was barely a whimper. No encore, I'm brought backstage and everyone tells me to go straight to the emergency room. Cody Votolato drives me and stays the whole time. The doctor said I either detached a muscle in my chest or have a viral infection in my lung. But either way, I'm suffering from extreme exhaustion and I need to stop drinking Red Bulls, eat more than one meal a day, and get more than three hours of sleep at night. I will have to call in a couple days to hear the results of my blood tests.

November 11, 2005--Memphis, TN--2:48 AM

Dinner with the Sire Records goon was brutal, the routine exhausting. I would be naive to think we were as special to them as he says we are. We are not a snowflake.

The lifestyle they offer is alluring. So much so that it blinds my sight at times. But pay attention to the mannerisms, the subtlety of speech, the nuances in phrasing. Watch how the conversation is led, when power is handed off, how carefully it is directed. Do not be afraid to drunkenly abandon the whole game, 'cause "fuck it" is a valid card to play. It is your trump

card, "I just don't care, try that one on
for size."

A&R from Sire is tall and skinny. His
face is skeletal. He has Alopecia and
wears a wig. He signed a list of bands
that all of us have heard of and respect
more than others because they get good
press but none of us actually listens to
which serves as credibility to us. He
reminds us all of Nosferatu.

I can't believe we're back in this situation again, drunkenly listening to an
A&R guy pitch his label. A&R pitches hard.
He's midway through his hour-long speech on
why we should sign to his label, compar-
ing our career to a river and I'm already
bored. Whoever offers us the most money
and complete artistic control wins, and
the rest can fuck off.

I want to sign to a major. I want to
take this shot.

———————

November 26, 2005--Richmond, VA--11:24 AM

Initial offers from both labels have
come in. The Sire offer is the best. It
totals 1.3 million dollars.

We had a band talk last night and all
agreed that even if Universal were to
match the offer, we want to sign with Sire/

Warner. Sire has a history we'd all be
proud to be a part of. It was home to the
Ramones, the Replacements, the Rezillos,
the Smiths, Echo & The Bunnymen, Madonna,
and so many more groundbreaking bands we
all respect. It's a gamble either way, but
it seems like a smart move.

Life comes hard, don't sell it cheap.

———————

December 4, 2005--NYC--4 AM

It was cold, standing outside in the
snow, hugging A&R from Universal. He tells
me how much he loves me and that no matter what label we choose to sign with, we
will still be friends but that if we don't
sign with his label, then he will probably
need some time before he can see me again.
I believe in the emotional connection he
says he feels with me and I love him back.
I wish that I felt confident in the rest
of his label. I wish they were offering
the kind of money that Sire is.

I was offered this advice recently: "Major
labels don't know how to sell 100k records.
They can sell 500k, they can sell a million,
if you're Green Day, they can even sell four
million. But that first 100k, that's why they
need you, that's why they're interested in
your band, because you've demonstrated that
you can sell that first 100k."

As of right now, we've sold around 30,000 copies of *Searching for a Former Clarity* and it's been out for four months.

I find the major label world attractive in the way that I do any other vice. It makes you feel great while making you hate yourself at the same time which makes you need it more until you can't remember any other way to feel love.

—————

December 15, 2005--Kansas City, KS--The Hotel Phillips--3:33 AM

We signed the contracts with Sire/Warner unceremoniously, just the four of us in a room at the Hotel Phillips, exhausted from the road after the last show of a three-month long tour that traveled to all 50 states.

The contract is daunting. The language is confusing. I think the lawyer is ripping us off. He's come down on his rate from $90,000 to $75,000 and we're told that we're supposed to feel like he's doing us a favor. All for negotiating just one contract!

The contract is a two-album record deal that totals over $1.5 million. What doesn't go to recording costs will be split equally among the four of us. I don't think any of us really comprehends the

weight or true ramifications of the deal
we are making. Still, I write out my signature without hesitation. After signing we
put our hands together in a pact, hailed
rock and roll, and headed down to the bar
for drinks.

Is Sire the right move? I don't know. Am
I alienating myself from friends by making
this decision? Yes. Is this all going to
end with me being alone? Yes. It doesn't
feel like an achievement, it feels like a
declaration of surrender.

Tour is over. In the morning we'll start
the long drive from Kansas City back to
Gainesville. We'll go through a Bank of
America drive-thru on University Avenue
and deposit our check, and then all go our
separate ways for the holidays.

After I drop everyone off at their
respective houses I will find my way to
my ex-wife. I will climb into bed next
to her. We will hold each other. We will
start to kiss. She'll take my shirt off.
I'll take her shirt off. Then I will flush
warm, break into a sweat and tell her we
need to stop.

I'll go there because I have nowhere and
no one else to go to. I'll leave because
it will not be where I belong. What once
felt so right will now feel all wrong.

If the punks were mad at us for signing to Fat Wreck Chords
before, surely they would want our blood now for signing to Sire.

And indeed, I started to hear blowback before even depositing the check into our band account, the amount of which was so huge that it made the bank teller do a triple-take and her jaw literally drop. I resented the punks for begrudging us this. We were finally successful. This was something I'd wanted ever since I was 5 and saw Madonna on TV, and I was being hated for it because of petty punk politics.

Looking at the bright side, it kept hitting me how incredible it was that the same guy who signed Madonna signed my band. I was starting to have dreams about her. Sometimes she and I were lovers, but sometimes we were just friends. I didn't want to wake up.

4. BORNE ON THE FM WAVES

We wanted to be huge, but knew deep down we never would be. That's the punk mentality, always shooting yourself in the foot before even taking the first step. We went into the major label experience expecting the worst, nervous about what promotional events we'd be pressured into committing to, or what tours we'd be signed up for. We didn't want them changing our DNA.

We were given a tour of the Warner offices, but left without understanding anything that had been said to us.

"So what exactly do you do here at the label?" I asked one guy who showed us around. I'd forgotten his name twice, and felt stupid asking again.

"I deal with MP3s and iTunes, digital media technology," he responded.

"What are you working on right now?"

"Well, actually, I'm really excited about this. There is this new drink coming out, it's a milk drink with different flavors, probably not that good for you. We're doing a deal with them for ringtones. You take a picture of the bottle in your hand on your cellphone and send it to a number and they in turn send you a ringtone. Like we hope to do for your band."

I didn't want to be a ringtone sold with shitty flavored milk.

I worried every day that by putting our names on the dotted line, we were signing our death warrant. I couldn't get that fucking lawyer's fee out of my head: $75,000 just for negotiating one contract. That was almost three times as much as we had made on our entire first record with Fat Wreck Chords.

The rest of the band seemed to mind less than I did. They had uses for their money. They were getting married, putting down payments on homes, adopting dogs, and buying big flat-screen TVs. Nothing beyond anyone's means, but starting adult lives, at least. Freshly divorced, the thought of that sort of mundane, domestic lifestyle was suffocating to me, yet at the same time, I was jealous. So determined was I to remain untethered that I didn't even have a permanent address.

I had put what few possessions I owned into a storage unit and was cashing in the thousands of hotel points we'd accrued on the road to live rent-free out of hotels on the swampy outskirts of Gainesville during the band's downtime between tours.

I've always loved hotels and am fascinated by them, even the most banal. There's a security to be found in the consistency of a good generic hotel chain. No matter where you go, at least this one thing remains the same. Non-offensive wall art like a framed sepia photograph of pine cones in a basket, complimentary toiletries lined up and waiting. Much like being in a punk band, hotel living is a suspended state of adolescence—someone there to change the bed sheets and bring you fresh towels every morning, no electric bill, free HBO, and room service at the push of a button. When it was time to leave for tour again, I would simply pack up my bags and check out. I lived like that for a year and a half.

Hotel living even made me healthier. I weaned myself off drinking and availed myself of the fitness center, sweating off the pounds with long runs on the treadmill. The only drawback was the extreme isolation. I had essentially exiled myself, trying to avoid my ex-wife and the bar life, but it gave me almost too much time for reflection. I had put so much of myself into the band, and even though I was proud of our success, underneath it, I felt alone. I felt envious of my bandmates and the lives they led outside of Against Me!. Andrew had his wife, James had his fiancée, and Warren had a whole group of friends and social life that he kept separate from the band. But I had no one. That loneliness ultimately led me to Heather.

I met Heather on the first day of tour. Against Me! was scheduled to do five weeks across the country in the spring of 2006 opening for Alkaline Trio, and she was selling their merch. More than their merch girl, Heather was the visual artist behind the designs on the band's T-shirts and album covers, including their iconic logo of a skull inside a heart, which countless fans have tattooed on their bodies.

It's a total cliché to put it like this, but I mean it when I say that Heather was truly the most beautiful woman I'd ever seen, the emphasis being on "woman." Whereas every other female I'd been with before was just a girl, she was a fully formed *woman*. An Egyptian-Canadian who grew up in a Detroit suburb, standing at six feet to my six feet and two inches, she was tall, dark, and mysterious. There was an exotic aura about her, and her gravity terrified me.

I was sitting off to the side of the stage, changing the strings on my guitar when she walked by and introduced herself. I told her I was excited about the tour and she agreed. If you blinked you'd miss the significance of this brief encounter, but I spent the rest of the day replaying it in my head.

The next night in Vegas, I asked if she wanted to get a drink at the bar. She dodged me with an excuse about having to meet up with her aunt. I took her word, although I thought she might be blowing me off. The next night, I talked her into having that drink, and the next night, and the night after that. Soon we were arm wrestling, then passing notes and stealing glances at each other throughout the day, making up excuses to walk by each other in the venue.

Heather and I spent the entirety of those weeks together. Alkaline Trio did the tour in a bus and we were in a van, but Heather started riding with us after a while. We'd sleep in the same bed, although we weren't having sex. Neither of us wanted to risk spoiling the spark between us. Mostly we would do the things two people do when they're crushing on each other—hold hands, stare into each other's eyes, eat apple pie at all-night diners and wash it down with stale coffee. I wrote her a song, but never played it for her. I penned the lyrics on a piece of paper, folded them up into a note, and slipped it to her just before doors opened at the NorVa in Virginia.

It turned out Heather was still halfway through a breakup with her ex back in Oakland, a guy named Smith. Smith was close friends with the members of Alkaline Trio and was roommates with their tour manager, Nolan. So out of solidarity to Smith, neither the band nor their crew took kindly to me spending so much time with her. Nolan would pull childish crap with us in retaliation, withholding the food and beer guaranteed in our rider, or shifting our set times around last minute as a power move.

"You have to go on an hour early tonight, right when doors open, because all of the band and crew want to get to our hotel early," he told us once.

I wasn't having any of it. "No, you dumb fuck," I said, waving our contract in his face. "It says right here that our set time is an hour after doors open."

Before one show in New York, Nolan got physical with Jordan who was tour managing us at the time, over our set time, shoving him to the ground. Jordan is tall and physically imposing, but he doesn't have a mean bone in his body. He's a total teddy bear. After I found out about the incident, I made it a point to call Nolan out on stage that night.

Nolan used to hide behind Alkaline Trio's amplifiers during their set and play a second guitar part along to the songs to fill in the sound, a move I thought was infinitely lame and unpunk. So I told the audience to "be sure and give an extra round of applause to Nolan, the hidden guitar player behind Alkaline Trio's amplifiers. He's been a little grumpy lately and needs the attention!"

Alkaline Trio's frontman, Matt Skiba, didn't like this and, armed with a crew behind him, he found me backstage after our set and told me his boys were going to beat my ass. None of my bandmates came to my defense, but our manager, Tom Sarig, got right up in Skiba's face.

"Fuck you, you fucking fuck, I will end you if you so much as breathe wrong on my artist."

Skiba backed down, but after that show, not one person from Alkaline Trio or their crew said a single word to me or even looked at me for the rest of the tour. Any working relationship I had with them was destroyed, but it only forced me and Heather closer. She told me she loved the way I stood up for myself, and that I was right in thinking Nolan was an asshole. She said I had a swagger that she found sexy.

Heather understood me. She knew what tour life was like; she lived the lifestyle too. She didn't judge me for the ways in which I'd learned to cope. I felt myself falling for her, and a singular thought struck me upon realizing this: *This person will kill me.*

April 3, 2006--Drive Day--Somewhere in New
Mexico

The tour manager is stoned behind the
wheel right now. The sun is shining. There
is endless desert to my right and there
are mountains to my left. There is no
other place in the world I would rather be
right now than here, riding shotgun while
driving east on I-10, listening to Ryan
Adams.

There is an art to touring in a
15-passenger van. The van is your shared
home away from home when you're on the
road (occupied by eight people in our particular case, four band and four crew).
You must be courteous of your fellow pas-
sengers. We've developed a set of unspoken
rules to make it work for us.

1. **The back two bench seats of a van
should always be reserved for sleeping.**
That way if a stop is made, those sleeping
can remain undisturbed in the back, no one
has to climb over them or push past their
extended legs. Some of the best sleep I
have ever gotten in my life has been on
the back bench seat of a 15-passenger van.

2. **If someone invites company along
on the road, that person must sit on the
front bench seat, passenger side.** This is
the worst seat in the van. You have nothing to lean on, nothing to prop your knees
up against. It's murder on your neck and

back. Already one of the sleeping benches
will have been sacrificed by having the
guest on board. The band and the crew
need rest. We are working. The guest is a
tourist in our world. Whoever invited said
guest should occupy the seat directly to
the left of the guest as this is the second least desirable seat in the van. The
host should never drive when a guest is in
company and under no circumstances should
the guest occupy the coveted shotgun seat,
especially if the host rudely chooses to
drive and especially if the host and guest
are a couple because no one wants to be
looking ahead at the road over two people
fawning over each other.

   3. **Guest should never, under any circumstances, occupy the rear bench seat while
host drives.** Hosts have assumedly invited
guests to spend time together so they better do just as much of that as possible.

April 11, 2006--Charlotte, NC

   Heather and I got matching tattoos of a
rat that Black Arm John The Roadie drew.
I'm a couple days deep into my crush on
her now. I've never met anyone like her.
I've never seen beauty that could match.
   We slept on the floor next to each other
at the Holiday Inn. We talked until sunrise.

We talked about our parents and agreed that
fathers suck. I never want to be a father.
I told her my theory that kids with parents
who stay together don't get cavities and
kids who come from a broken home do.

I want to touch her but I do not. I
want to kiss her but I do not. Waiting for
signal.

She told me that Neurosis was the best
show she's ever seen and that Lungfish is
her favorite band. I will now commit every
Lungfish song to memory.

April 13, 2006--Norfolk, VA

"Alright, boys, let's do this," Andrew
says before we take the stage. I'm not a
boy like him.

"We're all just normal dudes playing in
a rock and roll band." I'm not a normal
dude like Andrew, like the rest of them.

I wretch and crawl in my skin.

Door times were incorrectly advertised
and we take the stage to a half-empty
room. Seconds into our first song, the
stage lights go black and we are playing
in the dark. We play with overcompensating
anger for the rest of the set, which feels
good if not pointless.

Heather jumped into our van after the
show.

Together we polished off a bottle of
Jameson on the ride to the hotel.

Sitting on the hotel room floor in front
of the TV, we talked until everyone else
was asleep. Then it happened. Our hands
touched, our hands held, we kissed.

"I like you," she said. "I really like
you."

"Will you like me in the morning? You
aren't just drunk, are you?"

We slept next to each other on the bed.
In the morning I still like her.

Heather is by far the most beautiful
woman that I've ever kissed.

She is apart from the others.

April 18, 2006--NYC

I've managed to make enemies out of everyone in Alkaline Trio and all of their
crew. Most of them won't even look me in
the eye when we see each other around the
venues. They just walk by me in silence
looking the other way. Their tour manager
is a straight-up asshole and got physical
with Jordan yesterday, shoving him to the
ground over an argument about set times.
They clearly do not like that I'm hanging
out with Heather.

Heather and I have stayed at the Senton
Hotel for the past two nights. The band

has been staying at The Broadway Plaza
Hotel around the corner. There's an hourly
rate at the Senton and pornography is
already playing on the television when you
walk into a room but staying there with
her makes it my favorite hotel room that I
have ever been in.

Heather and I lay in bed and count the
cigarette burns in the blanket. We haven't
had sex, we've only made out. I could make
out with Heather forever.

Pill hangovers in the morning but I
haven't slept in days.

Cold sweats and shakes.

Were those Valiums 10s or 15s?

How many did I take again?

Pills to calm down.

Going to need some help to come back up.

I'm having a mild anxiety attack that's
on the verge of becoming a full blown
freak the fuck out.

This tour has shaken me.

Too much momentum.

She has shaken me.

This is all too much, too quick.

Fighting to stay in control of the
situation.

I don't want a girlfriend.

As the tour was ending and Heather and I were saying our
goodbyes, we made plans to meet up. We talked about taking
a road trip together through the South, driving someplace like

Savannah and exploring a city neither of us knew. But I ended up canceling on her before we had the chance.

Not only was I scared of the relationship between us going any further and setting me up for more heartbreak, I was overwhelmed by the pressure to make a hit record for Sire. Things were moving quickly on the new album—we were in the process of picking out a producer and scheduling recording sessions, and I was the only one in the band doing any writing. I had abandoned the idea of Against Me! being a full-band effort, and took on all the responsibility myself. I wanted this. I had waited my whole life for this. My credibility was on the line. I wasn't going to fuck that up over a girl.

Oftentimes on tour, the guys would go out and party through the night, and I'd be the lone weirdo who stayed behind at the hotel to write, trying to stay focused, trying to stay sober. This dynamic put a divide between me and the other members. Since I was writing the songs, I started to feel that I was entitled to the publishing rights to them, which led the rest of the band to feel that I was being a greedy asshole.

We were still in the honeymoon phase with the label, so I was letting things slide. It was a trade-off. While they were clueless about our band in certain regards, at least they were enthusiastic about us, assuring us that we were going to be huge and throwing a shit-ton of money into our efforts. They sent us a list of producers they suggested we work with for the new album. The only one that didn't make us all cringe was Butch Vig. Butch had produced some of the most influential records of the last 20 years, including Nirvana's *Nevermind*. I got set up on a call with him while we were in Leipzig, Germany, on our European tour.

Speaking on the phone with Butch was intimidating, but he told me he loved the demos and had ideas on how to push our vocal dynamics, going softer when called for. "It seems like you're always singing at a ten," he told me, before quickly apologizing. But my skin was thick. I wanted the criticism. "Just keep writing. You can never have too many songs," he encouraged before we hung up. "And don't be afraid to try new approaches as well. Venture outside your comfort zone!" I ended the call feeling sure that I wanted to work with him, although the rest of the band was still not convinced, unsure about how his background with bands like Nirvana and Smashing Pumpkins would translate to our punk sound. But I took his advice and kept writing songs as we trekked through Europe.

Some songs take time, some songs dissolve into nothing, and very rarely, a song will simply find you in the night. I wish there was a science to it, but there isn't. After treating ourselves to a €600 meal in France that included mussels and bottle after bottle of wine at a restaurant in our five-star Grand Hotel Des Thermes, a place fancy enough to make our crew stick out like eight sore thumbs, I walked along the shore of Saint Malo alone. I lit a joint and stared off at the horizon. A fully formed song—lyrics, melody, and all—crashed onto me like one of the incoming waves. It was the kind of moment you live for as a songwriter—true inspiration. A gift. I titled it "The Ocean," since I was staring out at sea.

The song was my interpretation of heaven, and how interconnected life is. In the middle of it, I included a line about wishing I'd been born a woman. I'd thrown very subtle hints at my dysphoria into Against Me! songs before, sprinkling in a few coded lyrics here and there over the years. Early on, in "The Disco before the Breakdown," I included the line: "And I know they're going to laugh at us when they see us out together holding hands like this." Being "together holding hands" was a metaphor for my relationship with "her." Later, in Searching for a Former Clarity's title track, I got a little bolder: "And in the journal you kept by the side of your bed, you wrote nightly in aspiration of developing as an author, confessing childhood secrets of dressing up in women's clothes, compulsions you never knew the reasons to." But "The Ocean" would be the most forthright. The thought of presenting the lyrics to the band made me uncomfortable. Still, I didn't want to change a word.

"If I could have chosen, I would have been born a woman. My mother once told me she would have named me Laura. I would grow up to be strong and beautiful like her. One day I'd find an honest man to make my husband."

May 22, 2006--Berlin, Germany

A&R is fucking clueless. We sent them a CD of demos we've recorded for the album. The CD included a cover of the Replacements song "Bastards Of Young."

"The songs are all great. I think 'Bastards Of Young' may be the best song you've ever written."

It's bad enough that they don't recognize that it's a cover. What's worse is that their label released the Replacements album the song is from. How am I supposed to take any of their opinions seriously? Why would I hand over any control to people who are so obviously clueless?

We leave the Warner offices and head to the venue, Tommy Weisbecker Haus, the squat show space named after a 23-year-old anarchist who was shot and killed by the police in front of the building in the 1970s. The cops claimed he was going for a gun. He was unarmed.

Ingo, the DIY promoter who has booked all our European tours so far, pulls me aside after sound check and tells me that he can no longer book the band.

"If your manager thinks he can find someone else to do the job better, then maybe you all should do this. If I do the tours then I do it my way and that's the way it is. I cannot work with the people you are working with now."

It's pointless arguing about it. All the things that Ingo hates in the music business are just becoming more and more a part of the way we do things. He doesn't make any money doing what he does, that is not his motivation. Call it "punk," call it "DIY," whatever you want to label it, in all of Ingo's stubborn glory he is a hero of mine. Thank you for everything.

Showtime finally. The muscles in my body relax, everything feels fluid and natural, like it's supposed to feel. The stage sounds good. The room feels right. The crowd is alive and breathing. Maybe getting a good night's sleep and not drinking the night before had something to do with it. Maybe it's the fact that the punks in the room are actually paying attention, actually fucking getting

it. Whatever it was, this was exactly the
kind of show I needed. The kind of show
where you feel a sense of fulfillment,
there was a reason you came here and this
was it.

Against Me! spent a month and a half in Europe, and I didn't
contact Heather while we were there. I made a point not to. I
needed to focus on writing, and thought she was a distraction.
We returned to America with two weeks to spare before spending the summer on the Warped Tour, the long-running traveling
punk-rooted festival. The lineup was stacked with established
acts like Less Than Jake, the Bouncing Souls, and Joan Jett.

Everyone knew who Joan was. Even the bigger bands on the
tour had grown up listening to her. We expected her to be far
removed and isolated from the rest of us rock wannabes, going
straight from tour bus to stage to tour bus, but instead, she acted
completely on our level and would always be down to hang out.
She had a BMX bike just like the rest of us that she would zip
around on through the festival grounds. She got stoned with us,
and was just generally the walking embodiment of cool in her
sunglasses and black tank top. On stage, she was full-on rock
and roll Joan Jett with her black leather pants and jacket. But
backstage, she hung around in camo shorts and sneakers.

NOFX was on the tour, too, and, since they were one of
the first bands to ever play the festival back in 1995, Fat Mike
was essentially the mayor of Warped Tour. We spent the next
two months under his wing, reaping all the benefits that came
with it.

Bus parking on Warped Tour is tricky. You're dealing with
a traveling circus with about a hundred buses rolling down the
highway. There was a person on Warped Tour whose specific job

was to coordinate where these buses parked each day. Conveniently, that person was NOFX's bus driver, Johnny. NOFX always got the parking spot they wanted, and Johnny made sure we got a spot next to them so that we could all party together. Set times on Warped Tour are chosen by lottery each morning to make it fair for all the bands, so that no one gets stuck always opening or always closing. But not for NOFX. They played at whatever time of day they wanted, based on how hungover Mike was. There were also lunch and dinner lines, where you'd have to queue up to get your meal. Members of NOFX were never at the end of the longest line and always cut straight to the front, if they even ate the cafeteria food at all. Something about it felt like juvenile high school behavior, but still, it was nice to sit with the cool kids for once.

I saw Heather on the first day of the tour.

June 15, 2006--Columbia, MD

We rolled in late for Warped Tour's "orientation day." I hate being late.

Walking around the festival grounds I spotted Heather unloading boxes of merch from the back of a truck, her hair pulled back into a ponytail. She was sweaty and beautiful.

I knew she got a job on the tour working for the Bouncing Souls, selling merch. She told me in advance but somehow still it was surprising to see her.

We spent the day together, exploring the woods surrounding the festival grounds. We walked to a shopping mall and bought squirt guns, remote control cars, a puzzle, and a Frisbee.

We went to the after-show party together. I felt awkward holding her hand while walking up to the scene of people at the welcoming party BBQ. That's what boyfriend and girlfriend do. Is she my girlfriend? Are we dating? We slept next to each other in the back bus lounge. We still haven't had sex.

I can't decide how I feel to be back in her company.

Anxiety, anxiety.

June 16, 2006--Columbus, OH

A 2001 Prevost, our first bus. Twelve bunks, two lounges, a kitchen, a bathroom, black leather upholstery, flat screen TVs, surround sound stereo system, hydraulic doors that open and close between each area at the push of a button. It's legit.

Our driver, Dale, arrived to pick us up in Florida wearing a shirt that reads "K-9 Sex Police--Doggystyle Unit" and while putting together a broom he bought at Walmart he informed us that the handle "would make a good nigger-beater." We're all terrified that we have to spend the next two months with him. I worry that Dale sees us all as kids and isn't going to take us seriously even though we're paying him.

It was an average first show of a tour, minus the fact that our set was right in between the Buzzcocks and Joan Jett. What a sweet spot to be in!

First shows are never that good. You're still trying to find your rhythm. Playing in the sun drains you. Being constantly surrounded by people and bombarded by noise all day long drains you.

Butch Vig is coming to the show tomorrow. It will be our first time meeting in person.

The first mission of every day on Warped Tour is to find the nearest Porta-Potty while they're still relatively more clean and fresh than they will be by the end of the day. Baking in the sun, the Porta-Potty is a sweat box, the toilet seat burns your ass when you sit on it. When you get up, your ass leaves an outline of sweat.

June 22, 2006--Driving to Jacksonville, FL

Heather and I had sex. She was checking into her hotel room when I came down to the lobby to meet everyone for breakfast. I skipped breakfast and went with her to her room instead.

It is indescribable how salty her skin
tastes when kissed. It makes my sun-burned
lips sting.

Protection was used. Nothing would
destroy me more than harming Heather.

After lying in bed all morning we found
an arcade and played air hockey, video
games, and skee-ball. Then ate dinner at a
shitty chain restaurant.

Her ex-boyfriend is on this tour. He
introduced himself to me, said it would be
stupid for us to avoid each other all tour.
He introduced himself to everyone in the
band and all significant others. Despite
how cool it is of him, I find myself just
feeling agitated and annoyed having to
experience the situation in any way at all.

I can't tell what Heather expects from
me. I think I'm wasting my time. I'm just
a rebound. What happens when the summer's over? I'm just the next guy, the guy
before the next.

July 11, 2006--Ventura, CA

You are never alone on this tour. There
is always someone outside of the band
circle around that needs entertaining or
hosting. There is always a tour of the bus
to give or a cold drink in need of offering. It's exhausting always being on.

The manager's assistant has been riding with us the past couple days. She
accompanied me to L.A. for press yesterday. Crashed the rental car drunk through
the hotel security gate coming back. We
laughed wildly as we settled into a parking space. No one saw it happen. Then she
turns to me and we're kissing hard.

"Wait, no, stop, I can't do this with
you anymore."

"What do you mean?"

"I think I may have a girlfriend now."

She stormed away furious. This will not
make working together easy. I don't know
what I'm doing.

When we arrived backstage before our set
time today the stage manager told me that
everyone had a gift for me.

"What is it?"

They pulled out the security gate
arm I had crashed through with the car,
wrapped in a bow. They had seen the whole
thing and thought it was hilarious.

———————

July 18, 2006--Vancouver, BC

I'm already three big rails deep and
it's not even 8 PM.

Immediately after I get high, James
comes on the tour bus and tells me that
Erin Burkett, Fat Mike's wife and co-owner

of Fat Wreck Chords, wants to talk to me
outside. I had been warned to expect this.

Erin feels wronged by us leaving Fat
Wreck Chords and she wanted to let me
know. She also told me how much she dis-
likes the manager. She doesn't think there
is any good in his heart and that he
doesn't act with our best interests in
mind. There's nothing I can say in reply
to her, both because I can't unclench my
jaw to speak and because I think she's
right on all counts.

Received word that Butch is definitely
producing the next album. The label has
approved all budgets and studio time is
being booked in L.A. for October.

Heather takes a note out of her pocket,
presses it into my hand and then presses
my hand against my chest. "Tom" is written
in rub-on letters on the outside of the
small manila envelope. Inside of the envelope is a small print of a brown bird on a
twig, a branch with a banner underneath it
with "more please" written on it.

More please.

I'm surrendering.

————————

July 22, 2006--Driving to SLC

Day off in the time capsule that is
Butte, Montana.

At a bar called the Pleasure Palace,
Bubba, the ex-con/Vietnam vet/Hell's Angel,
tells me, "This is a hard place to live.
You gotta be careful. Don't never back
down. You hear what I'm saying? Don't never
back down. Once they see you back down,
it's all over."

Heather and I do a shot of tequila with
Bubba and he introduces us to his friends.
I try to buy Bubba another shot as we are
leaving but he refuses. I could see the
wobble in his step and hear the slur in
his speech. Bubba was at his limit and he
knew it. I should be so lucky as to know
my limits some day.

Heather and I check into a room at the
Hotel Finlen, modeled after the Waldorf
Astoria in NYC. Lying naked together in
bed, I caress the length of her torso.

"Tell me how you want me to fuck you."

"Will you fuck me without a condom?"

I break out in a cold sweat.

———

August 9, 2006--Driving to Virginia Beach, VA

Joan Jett watched our set. She came up
to me backstage after we were done. I was
trying to catch my breath and she offered
me a bottle of ice-cold water. She asked
if we would be down to come by her bus
later on and record an interview for her

radio show. I was leaning over and she
knelt down to talk to me. She usually
wears a lot of eye makeup but she wasn't
wearing any right then. She looked so
beautiful. Beautiful Joan Jett, a true rock
star.

James and I did the interview together
on Joan's bus in the evening after the
last band had finished playing for the
day. It was fun hanging out with her and
Kenny, her manager. She's usually so full
of swagger but when it was just the four
of us, I could tell that she's still a kid
at heart.

When the interview was over Joan gave
us each a hug. I wanted to hug Joan Jett
forever.

Taking Butch's advice, I wrote as many songs as I could for
the new record. In total, I entered our recording session with 30
songs, 10 of which would make the album. "The Ocean" made
the cut, but barely. The label hated it, but I insisted we keep it.
It would sneak onto the very end as the album's last song. We
spent the fall in Los Angeles, recording at Paramount Studios,
which had no relation to the movie studio but was still right
down the street from it.

The band stayed at an extended-stay furnished apartment
complex called the Oakwoods, the same place Nirvana stayed
while recording *Nevermind,* and the spot where just two years
prior Rick James was found dead of cardiac failure. I'd always
wanted to attend the Sunday pool parties there, but given that

the complex seemed to consist of aspiring actors and porn stars, I figured I'd be better off avoiding them. We each had our own studio apartment and were spread out across the complex. It was comfortable and clean, the first time I found myself actually enjoying myself in Los Angeles.

There was a dry-erase board hanging on the wall of our rehearsal space with a list of bands occupying the other rooms written on it. We were in studio 3. The two studios below us were blocked off for a band: "Guns and Roses." Ten-year-old me was doing somersaults.

October 9, 2006--Los Angeles, CA

I haven't been able to get Heather out of my head. I have fallen in love and it's horrible, the absolute worst thing that could happen to me right now. I want to be focused on the band, on the album we're making. Heather is a distraction. She makes me think about marriage and having kids. It's so completely out of control. I'm guessing that if I were to bring any of this stuff up it would scare her off.

We talked for over an hour tonight. I hate the way I speak. I hate the sound of my voice, my phrasing and my tone. It's not me. I feel detached from it, like I'm playing a character. I don't know how to say what I'm really feeling. I don't think I should say what I'm really think-ing, that I've never liked the name given to me, that I've never felt comfortable in

this body. The only time I'm happy is when
I am on stage. I don't like the person
that I have become. I don't like the way
that I treat other people.

I slept until 1:40 PM today. I don't
remember what time I went to sleep. I
don't remember how I got back to my apartment. My mental state is slipping. I have
to do something.

I need coffee.

———————

October 18, 2006--Los Angeles, CA

Third day of tracking and I've yet to
record an actual note of music. The first
day was spent dealing with some kind of
signal phase issue, the second day was all
drums. Warren must have tried out 20 different snares, one of them being "Big Red,"
the snare drum used on the Guns N' Roses
songs "November Rain" and "Don't Cry." We
are all in agreement that we love this
studio, that we love all the people working on the album, that we love having this
many resources available to us. It makes
us laugh to think though that anyone has
ever commented that any of our past albums
have sounded too "overproduced."

They take you out to dinner and tell
you it's going to be an amazing album.
They've got "a five-star *Rolling Stone*

review feeling." They make a toast to the producer they've always dreamed of working with, to the band, and to the future. You want to believe, 'cause wouldn't it be fun?

Remember, there's no such thing as a free meal.

Heather flew in a couple nights ago. We've decided to move in together, get a place in Gainesville. We plan on starting to look for a place in December, when I'm done with the album. I'm nervous and scared, but it's good. I feel like every day there's amazing progression in our relationship. We've talked about exes, a subject I usually avoid. She asked me a couple things about my marriage. She said some things about her past relationships. Nothing I can't handle.

———

October 26, 2006--Los Angeles, CA

The studio day is over before you know it. You're buzzed inside in the morning, stepping out of the sunshine and then you're buzzed out at night walking out into darkness.

I stopped after the first vocal take through "The Ocean" and asked Butch and everyone else in the control room if the lyric to the second verse was too weird. Should I change it?

"If I could have chosen, I would have been born a woman. My mother once told me she would have named me Laura."

I made a joke about being really high when it was written and tried to explain that the lyrics were just stream of consciousness, that I don't really mean anything by them.

Zero response. Nothing. No feedback, complimentary or critical. Butch finally says, "No it's cool, go with it."

We could hear Fiona Apple's voice coming down the hallway through the cracked door of the room she was rehearsing in. I wish I had a voice like hers. I wish our room was more soundproof so no one walking by could hear me sing. I wish we weren't listening to the new Killers album like a bunch of fucking dorks as we pulled up to park outside the space they are practicing in.

Lying in bed next to Heather, I find myself so very painfully self-aware. I shouldn't be with her. I need to be alone right now.

———

November 16, 2006--Los Angeles, CA

Seymour Stein is a dinosaur, a living breathing music industry dinosaur. I must admit I first heard his name through

a Belle & Sebastian song. He started Sire
Records. He signed Madonna and the Ramones
among so many other world-changing bands.
The music history of the label he built is
a big reason why we wanted to be a part
of Sire Records.

We were doing overdubs on the song
"White People For Peace" when a voice
comes on the intercom announcing that Seymour Stein was here to see us. Was this
a joke? Sure enough, Seymour slowly walks
into the control room and introduces himself. He shakes our hands and we exchange
introductions.

"Can I hear some songs?" he asks, breaking the awkward silence.

"Sure. Let's just finish up these overdubs first," says Butch.

I did my best to finish up the overdubs but was nervous with Seymour standing
right beside me listening to me play. I'm
not sure if I nailed the part but Butch
let it go after a couple more takes and
asked the engineer to put it on stun volume for playback.

"Johnny Ramone would have either loved
it or hated it!" Seymour says after the
song finishes.

"It's an upper and a downer at the same
time," adds Butch.

"Sounds like a speedball," says Seymour.

December 14, 2006--Los Angeles, CA

The Sire Records team came into the
studio today. They listened to the eight
songs that we had ready to play them rough
mixes of. The songs played, they gave us
a thumbs up, told us it sounded great,
and then left quickly. All except for A&R.
A&R had suggestions. The idea was proposed that we edit the length of "Thrash
Unreal" to make it shorter. Some lyric
changes, written by A&R, are suggested,
as are vocal harmonies. Listening to A&R
talk makes me want to punch a hole in a
wall.

I don't want their personal touch on
our music. I'm at the end of my rope with
compromising.

You're always a baby band in the major
label world until you're a has-been,
unless you blow up. Everyone makes me feel
like I'm just an asshole they just put up
with.

I said my ex-wife's name last night
while Heather and I were having sex.
Heather didn't say anything. I'm hoping
she maybe didn't hear it but how could she
not? I wasn't thinking about my ex-wife
at the time. I was there, mentally present
with Heather, it just happened. What the
fuck is wrong with me?

December 20, 2006--Los Angeles, CA

I left the studio tonight with a CD of 14 rough mixes, the songs that will become our fourth full-length album. I am alone in celebrating the last day of tracking; the rest of the band left back for Florida a couple days ago. Just me, a pint of Guinness, and cable TV. The future is uncertain, but my time spent here in L.A. will always remain a happy memory. Thank you, Butch.

Goodbye, Los Angeles. Goodbye, Oakwoods Apartments.

We've been offered a $400,000 publishing advance by Warner/Chappell publishing. The lawyer says it's "unheard of for a young band to get offered that much." I asked the manager how many albums we would have to sell to recoup. We would have to sell 450,000, just shy of gold.

I don't trust the manager or the lawyer. They're just looking to get paid. They'd leave me high and dry if the band were to fall apart. I'm going to turn down the advance.

I'm flying to south Florida in the morning to spend Christmas with my mom and brother.

It was the first day of 2007, and Heather and I were both a gin-and-tonic deep at Jacqueline's, a dive bar in Chicago. We'd had drinks there during the tour on which we met, talking about nothing, talking about everything.

She was caressing my hand in hers, spinning my ring around my finger. It was an old ring my mother had given me, emblazoned with our family's Irish Catholic crest. I guess I wore it for its sentimental value.

Heather gently slipped it off of my finger and played with it, examining it in her fingertips. She slid it onto the index finger of her left hand where it fit loosely. It moved down the line to her middle finger. She removed it again and then held the opening to the tip of her ring finger, looking up at me, not saying anything as she slowly slid it down toward her hand.

I could see the thought in her eyes, the "yes" waiting behind her lips. This was the part where I was supposed to ask her. As if on cue, "Come Sail Away" came on the jukebox and put a lump in my throat. It just came out of my mouth.

"Will you marry me?"

5. THRASH UNREAL

We were married on April 11, one year to the date of our first kiss. We told no one. I'd be lying if I said I wasn't nervous.

The South Beach Satellite Courthouse was all but empty except for a bus driver protesting a ticket and a young woman sitting in wait.

A middle-aged Cuban woman named Doris performed the service for $30. Doris's thick accent made her English hard to decipher but completely charming. Not fully understanding what she was saying, we held back laughter as we kept jumping the "I do" part. We didn't plan on telling friends or family that we were already married, and agreed to have a more formal wedding at the end of the year, when there was more time.

We drank champagne and shared a salad and French fries. We made love in our hotel room, the first time as man and wife, and then went swimming in the Atlantic Ocean. She told me it was the happiest day of her life. I still have the picture of her in a silver leopard print bikini, jokingly posing for me on the beach like a 40s pin-up model. It's a black-and-white Polaroid, the kind you have to physically pull from the camera and hope the film actually develops. I used to keep that picture pinned to the roof of my bus bunk. Heather, still smiling from that day's private adventure, frozen in time.

Just before she fell asleep in my arms, I whispered in her ear that I hoped I would never stop exciting her.

———

We called our major label debut *New Wave*. The title was supposed to suggest rebirth, the beginning of a new chapter in the band's history, but it all seemed cursed from the start.

"We can control the medium. We can control the context of presentation..."

We rushed to put a last-minute album cover together, having blown our budget hiring a photographer to take photos for it that no one ended up liking. Compositionally, the shots were fine, but we wanted something that expressed youthful renewal. Since the subjects in the pictures looked freezing cold as they were taken in Germany in February, it didn't make sense to use them for a summer release.

To kill time in the studio between takes, I had been working on a stencil design based on a picture of a snarling Florida panther photocopied from *National Geographic* magazine. Using an X-Acto knife and a Sharpie, I had meticulously traced and cut out the image. With no other artwork options, I insisted we use it. The punks could call me a sellout for abandoning the scene we had started in and signing with a big, dumb corporate label, at least I could say I remained true to my art, designing cover artwork the same way I did when I lived with my mom.

Two weeks before its scheduled release date in the summer

of 2007, as we were touring through Europe, headed to Munster, Germany, we got word that the album had leaked online. The label panicked and went into damage control mode, scrambling to corrupt the files, but it was too late. It was already out there. Album leaks and declining album sales were still a new phenomenon at the time. I didn't want anyone punished for piracy, but at the same time, I did feel that control had been stolen from me.

Sometimes the leak worked to our advantage. People in the crowd that night were already singing along to songs that weren't even out yet. Seeing the immediate enthusiasm for our efforts felt reassuring, like we had made a smart decision signing to a major and were on the right path. But as usual, for every one fan we gained from the exposure, it seemed like we lost two because of our corporate partner.

After that night's show, an anarchist squatter cornered me outside the venue. As if reading from a script, he ripped right into me. He didn't like the venue we played. He didn't like our new songs. He didn't like how many amplifiers we had on stage. He didn't like that we were traveling in a tour bus and not a van. He didn't like that we signed contracts with a record label. He didn't like that I didn't speak in between songs when we played, and said that I wasted a chance to inform people. He told me that he had originally planned to storm the show with fellow squatters, but when they saw that tickets were only €10, they decided it wasn't enough money to storm a show over.

Interactions with bitter crustpunks like this were becoming more common. Seeing them outside our shows made me apprehensive since they were usually only there to protest us or vandalize our bus. They'd sneak into the venues and spit on us from the front row or hurl bottles at us from the back.

Sometimes after our sets, if we would hang out and share our beer with them, they'd give us a pass. "I was ready to write you assholes off," one of them told me outside our bus, taking a sip from a 40-ounce of Olde English Malt Liquor. "But I guess you're still cool in my book." We talked about punk and Crass records until his friend picked a fight with a passerby and all the crusties piled on. I took the opportunity to slip away, back to the bus. As I looked back, the guy was standing with his back against a wall, a broken beer bottle in each hand, bleeding profusely from his face.

We came back to the United States in desperate need of some time to relax. Instead we jumped into the last tour we should have been doing at the moment, co-headlining with Mastodon, and supported by Cursive, Planes Mistaken for Stars, and These Arms Are Snakes. Mastodon were metal behemoths who partied as hard as they rocked. They set a bar for substance intake so ridiculously high that none of us could possibly keep up, though that didn't stop me from trying. A show in Milwaukee had to be cancelled because Brent from Mastodon was too fucked up from the night before.

By the start of the second week, I was decimated. I woke up in Denver with my nostrils sealed completely shut and running a temperature of 101 degrees. I felt like walking death. I had to cancel a major photo shoot that a label representative had specifically flown out to accompany me to. Instead of going, I asked the tour manager to call me a "rock doc." I had come to rely on the trick J. Robbins had taught me while making *Searching*: what to do when you absolutely have to get through a show but aren't sure you physically can. A doctor will come make a house call to the venue and open up their black bag and give you whatever you want to get through the show, a shot of cortisone to reduce swelling of the vocal cords and a shot of vitamin B12, both needles stabbed into the butt, maybe a couple Valium for nerves, and you're ready to rock. But I wasn't as ready as I thought.

Two songs from the end of that night's set, my face went white as I felt my stomach drop. Still strumming through the chords of the song, I rushed to the side of the stage to find our guitar tech, Matt Steinke.

"Matt, you gotta get me a fucking box!" I shouted over the amp.

"What?"

"A box! I need one right now!"

He could tell by the panic in my face that I wasn't joking. All he could produce on emergency notice was a FedEx mailer box. I grabbed it from him and ducked behind the road cases, dropped my pants, shat in the box, and was back up and playing before the song ended. No one even saw me. We finished the set and I carried the box off stage with me. The show must go on, truly.

It was a terrible tour to lead into a record release. A good time, sure, but it probably took 10 years off my life. We could have used a month off afterward to recover, but we had other obligations. We were moving fast, jumping immediately into a press tour and filming a music video for the album's single, "Thrash Unreal."

The label suggested a director whose idea for the video was a satire of the show *America's Next Top Model*. Instead of models, it would be a show about drug users called *America's Next Top Junkie*. The video director assured me it would "break the fourth wall" and "have a humanness to it." I hated the idea of judging people for their addictions. I told him I wanted to do something that explored gender and volunteered to cross-dress in it, appearing en femme, supported by some sort of narrative. I guess this was me trying to push the limits of how far I could take my suppressed identity. They told me I couldn't.

Instead, we compromised on an idea from another director that felt forced and stale. It would depict the band playing in a basement underneath an upscale party. The partygoers donning tuxedos and cocktail dresses would spill wine that would rain down from the ceiling and drench us.

Once we begrudgingly conceded to the idea, we submitted a list of all the equipment the band needed, because why not milk it for some free gear? But when we showed up to the set in Los Angeles to film, half of it was missing. There was no hardware for the drum kit, no cymbal stands, and no heads on the kick drum. There wasn't even a stool for Warren to sit on. The director told him to squat down on a crate and just pretend he was playing a full drum kit so we could start shooting, and that he would make sure to edit around it so no one would notice. I couldn't see this going well.

I saw the writing on the wall early: We were screwed and were wasting our money, almost $100,000, on a disastrously bad video. But there was no way I was going to admit that to the band. After all, this awful compromise was one I had to fight for. So when the director told us to all run laps around the building before we started shooting, I ran the fastest. When he told me to take my shirt off for the shoot, I did not protest.

We were also pressured into asking fans to appear as extras since the director went over budget and needed people to work for free. I watched the video crew treat them like shit all day, leaving them waiting in a cramped storage area for hours with no food or drinks. We had to sneak them soda and chips so they wouldn't starve, and a few beers for their troubles.

The director had a couple of his stuntperson jock friends come down and make sure there were at least some people in the party scenes that were aggressive and out of control. One of them jumped off a table and accidentally kicked a fan square in the face. The band stayed with her and helped ice her bleeding lip, but no one from the film crew even apologized. The feeling that I was exploiting my own fans bothered me more than anything.

Our scenes were completed in five hours. We shot 12 takes, getting drenched in fake red wine coming out of an overhead sprinkler system each time. Our skin was dyed pink from head to toe by the time we were done, but the A&R still urged us to be interviewed on camera for behind-the-scenes commentary on the making of the video. The director also wanted to be interviewed and, like a total asshole, insisted on lying on a white leather couch while doing so. I didn't have high hopes for how the video would turn out, but I kept that to myself since the collective morale was already so low.

There were a lot of things I was burying deep in the back of my mind—the angry crusties who were jumping down our throats over our every move, the frustration with the label making us out to be something we weren't, lingering guilt from my first marriage collapsing and the wife and child I abandoned, the dysphoria I was fighting to get under control, and all of my spiraling addictions. We spent a week between Los Angeles and New York doing media. I could feel it all crashing down around me.

July 12, 2007--NYC

After the interview at FUSE TV I find myself standing in silence next to Marilyn Manson, pissing in urinals in the green room restrooms. We turn to each other.
"How's it going?"
"Not bad."
Neither of us wash our hands. He leaves the restroom before me.
Anxiety attack in the car service van on the drive to our record release dinner. Suddenly everything just feels wrong and I want it all to stop. Get me out of this fucking van. Get me away from these

fucking people. I want to kick open the doors and run off into the NYC night.

Our performance on *Conan* feels like a success. We were finished before I even realized we had started. I left filled with adrenaline. Conan hung out in the green room with us, cracking jokes after the show. Out of all the late night hosts we've met, he is the most persona-ble. We all watched the broadcast together back at the hotel in the tour manager's room.

I'm dying to know what first week sales figures are. It doesn't determine success of the work to me but I am aware that Sire has a bottom line, and album sales will determine the politics behind our working relationship going forward. The number will have influence over the course my life will take for years to come.

———

July 14, 2007--Los Angeles, CA--Renaissance Hollywood Hotel

We don't make it back to the Milford Plaza Hotel until 4 AM. Heather and I stay up for another hour finishing off our white drugs. It's good coke, the kind that makes you open up and talk, which Heather and I do until the sun rises.

The *SPIN* Magazine loading dock show at
Milk Studios is surreal. It feels like a
real event, like there was no place cooler
in the city at that moment. Seymour Stein
brings Bill Paxton, who immediately walks
up to me and James when he arrives backstage, congratulating us on the new album.

Paxton stands on the side of the stage
while we play, taking pictures on his camera phone, and, after the show, leads us
all to a bar a friend of his owns. He
buys round after round of drinks.

I hold court with a group of friends in
the corner of the bar, passing around a
bag of blow taking turns doing key bumps.

Heather and I get an hour's worth of
sleep before lobby call to make our flight
from NYC to LA.

Playing an acoustic show in a record
store was the very last thing that I
wanted to do when we got to LA. I was
dreading it. I wanted to sleep for a day
straight. On the van ride to Backside
Records we start passing around a bottle
of Jameson.

Whiskey will carry us through if
nothing else will. I feel loose when we
step up onto the small stage in the center
of the store. The bottle continues to be
passed around in between songs. There's
a handful of label suits in the room
but everything feels casual and relaxed.

People shout and sing along. We trade heck-
les back and forth with the crowd. I could
have played all night long.

———————————

July 28, 2007--Seattle, WA

Capitol Hill Block Party. Our set is
sandwiched between Aesop Rock and Spoon.
Whenever we play a new song, punks in the
audience stop dancing and stand still while
holding their middle fingers in the air. It
makes me wish we only played new songs.

Tonight was the first time I have ever
been flashed by a female while on stage.
There she was, sitting on shoulders, holding her shirt and bra up. I wish I could
be that kind of frontman but it's not me.
I felt embarrassed for her.

Ended the night in the back lounge of
the tour bus doing blow until the sun came
up with Har Mar Superstar, Rocky Votolato,
and the festival promoter.

———————————

The tour bus was waiting for me in the parking lot of the Leon
County Jail at 4 AM after I was processed, charged with battery,
bonded out, and released on $500 bail. Radar, our bus driver on
that run, gave me a kind nod and smile as I jumped on board
with a sigh.

In my cell, I had been seated next to a bleary-eyed man

MY FIRST SCHOOL PHOTO.

ME, MY BROTHER MARK, MY DAD, MY MOM. THE ONLY PHOTO I HAVE OF THE FOUR OF US TOGETHER.

ME (WITH A MOHAWK) AND DUSTIN PRACTICING IN HIS PARENTS' BASEMENT WITH OUR FIRST PUNK BAND, THE ADVERSARIES.

HAVING BEEN KICKED OFF THE SHOW BILL AT THE STATE THEATRE, KEVIN AND I DECIDED TO SET UP AND PLAY ON THE SIDEWALK OUT FRONT, ACCOMPA- NIED BY ANYONE WHO WANTED TO JOIN IN.

KEVIN (LEFT) AND ME ALL DRESSED UP TO GO TO A PARTY. I WAS JEALOUS OF HOW GOOD HE LOOKED IN THE DRESS.

IT TOOK ME YEARS TO PERFECT THE PUNK SNEER. HERE I AM AT 19 YEARS OLD STILL GETTING IT DOWN.

KEVIN, JAMES, DUSTIN (IN FRONT), AND ME ON THE TOUR THAT WOULD END IN A VAN ACCIDENT. BEING A BAND FROM FLORIDA, WE WOULD GET OVEREXCITED ABOUT SOMETHING LIKE THE NOVELTY OF SNOW. SAID EXCITEMENT WOULD WEAR OFF ONCE WE REALIZED THE VAN HAD NO HEAT.

BROKEN DOWN SOMEWHERE ON THE ROAD AND WAITING FOR A TOW TRUCK.

THE TOW YARD WRECKAGE OF OUR FORD ECONOLINE VAN AFTER BEING REAR-ENDED BY A SEMI TRUCK AND ROLLING MULTIPLE TIMES.

FIRST SHOW OF OUR SUMMER TOUR WITH FIYA AT THE DIY SHOW SPACE TIGHT POCKETS. DUSTIN'S LAST TOUR WITH THE BAND. WE HAVE ALWAYS FELT LOVED AND AT HOME IN ATHENS, GEORGIA.

MYSELF, ANDREW (IN THE CORNER), JAMES, JORDAN, AND GUNNAR (OUR FRIEND AND DRIVER) ALL GETTING SETTLED IN OUR SLEEPING BAGS FOR A LONG COLD NIGHT SLEEPING IN A SQUAT IN ITALY.

SHIRTLESS, DRUNK, AND GETTING CARRIED AWAY QUITE LIT-ERALLY, THROWN OVER ANDREW'S SHOULDER.

THE ONLY PHOTO I HAVE OF ME AND CC. OUR RELATIONSHIP WAS SUPPOSED TO BE A SECRET, SO WE WOULD HAVE NEVER PURPOSELY POSED FOR A PHOTO TOGETHER.

A LEGENDARY NIGHT OF SHIRTS OFF, BEER DRINKING, AND ARM WRESTLING (YES, THIS KIND OF SHIT ACTUALLY HAPPENS ON TOUR) WITH PLANES MISTAKEN FOR STARS AND NO CHOICE. LEFT TO RIGHT: MATT BELLINGER, ME, JORDAN KLEEMAN, GARED O'DONNELL, MOWGLI, AND ADAM VOLK.

A CONTEMPLATIVE MOMENT ONSTAGE AT THE STATE THEATRE IN SAINT PETERSBURG, FLORIDA. A VENUE I GREW UP SEEING OTHER BANDS PLAY AT, IT STILL TO THIS DAY STRIKES ME AS SPECIAL TO PERFORM THERE.

THE COVER PHOTO FOR OUR *WE'RE NEVER GOING HOME* TOUR DOCUMENTARY: ANDREW AND I JUMPING UP FOR A MIDAIR HIGH FIVE.

AFTER FINISHING MIXING THE *NEW WAVE* ALBUM AT ELECTRIC LADY STUDIOS IN NYC, BUTCH VIG INSISTED WE ALL GO TO THE HAT STORE ACROSS THE STREET AND BUY CELEBRATORY HATS.

BACKSTAGE AT STARLAND BALLROOM IN SAYERRVILLE, NEW JERSEY, WITH BRUCE SPRINGSTEEN AND HIS SON EVAN.

THE FOUR OF US FEELING AND LOOKING COMPLETELY DRAINED AFTER PLAYING A SCORCHING-HOT DAYTIME SET AND TWO YEARS ON TOUR IN SUPPORT OF THE *NEW WAVE* ALBUM.

STILL NEWLY IN LOVE, SITTING ON STEPS OUTSIDE OF A VENUE ENTRANCE IN BERLIN.

WANDERING AROUND DOWN-TOWN BIRMINGHAM, ALABAMA, WITH PHOTOGRAPHER RYAN RUSSELL TAKING PUBLICITY PHOTOS AROUND THE TIME OF MY 2008 SOLO RELEASE *HEARTBURNS*. RYAN HAS LONG BEEN MY FAVORITE PHOTOGRAPHER TO WORK WITH.

THE ONE-OF-A-KIND POPE OUTSIDE A GAS STATION ON OUR FIRST TOUR WITH HIM.

FLEXING OUR MUSCLES AND EATING OATMEAL AT HOME IN SAINT AUGUSTINE, FLORIDA.

INGE, ATOM, ME, AND JAMES ON THE ROAD TOURING FOR *TRANSGENDER DYSPHORIA BLUES.* THOSE WERE SHOWS I HONESTLY NEVER THOUGHT WOULD HAPPEN.

dressed only in a pair of sweatpants and a white tank top who went by the name of Mills. "All the prisons gonna start farming out inmates' body parts for profit," he told me. He seemed like a seasoned veteran of the system, and I didn't question his wisdom. I nodded my head, listening to him talk, but mostly my mind wandered, lost in regret. I thought about what a stupid mistake I'd made and how much hell was in store for me.

Earlier that day, Heather and I walked to a coffee shop in Tallahassee that shared a parking lot with the Beta Bar, a venue Against Me! was scheduled to play that night, a place we had played regularly. We ordered tea and I walked toward the back to use the restroom, where I saw a bulletin board on the wall with various flyers and notes tacked to it. One was a write-up for our show cut from a newspaper. Someone had taken a pen to it, cross-ing out all our eyes with Xs and scrawling the word "sellout" across my forehead. I tore it down, crumpled it up, and threw it in the trash. When I turned around, there was a punk right in my face.

"What'd you do that for?" he snarled.

"This was insulting to me, so I threw it out," I told him.

"Who the fuck do you think you are? This is our space, not yours." He turned his back to me, walking to take his seat at the counter.

I chased after him. "I'm a fucking human being, and I don't know you. Why are you treating me like this?"

He sat in front of his coffee, ignoring me. "What's your prob-lem?" I pressed.

"As far as I'm concerned, this conversation is over," he said, flashing me a smug look.

As far as I was concerned, it wasn't. I snapped. At that moment, this guy was every person who'd ever called me a sellout, every punk in the crowd who'd given me the finger, every asshole who'd ever slandered my band's name in a fanzine.

He raised his cup to take a sip but I knocked it out of his

hand before it reached his lips, sending coffee splattering in all directions. I grabbed him by the back of the neck and slammed his face down, pinning his cheek against the wet counter. I was completely blacked out. I don't know what I would have done at that moment if I hadn't been torn off of him by some people who started taking shots at me.

What I didn't realize was that later that night, this coffee shop was holding a protest show to counter the Against Me! show next door. Most of the people there knew who I was, and they tried to wrestle me to the ground. To me, they were just strangers throwing punches, but they knew my name. Every blow that landed on my body was a mark of revenge on behalf of the punk scene. It was a head-butt that brought me back to reality. It wasn't that it hurt; it was just that the idea of getting head-butted was so ridiculous that it snapped me to my senses.

"Just let me go," I told them.

"I'm going to release your arms," I heard someone behind me say. "If you hit me, I swear to God I'll fucking kill you."

"Sure, bro," I thought. "You're going to kill me. Right."

I had no idea what Heather was thinking as we left the scene. She said nothing. We walked in silence along the nearby railroad tracks until it was time to get back to the venue. There were two police cars waiting in the parking lot when we arrived.

I walked up to the first officer I saw, introduced myself, and asked if they were looking for me. He informed me they had to arrest me, but gave me a choice: I could go straight to jail or play the show first. I chose to play, setting myself up for a terrible performance. I was distracted throughout the whole set by an inner rage of defeat and the dread of what was waiting for me when it was over. I had been wrung through the legal system before and knew the long, arduous process I was in for.

After the show was over, I changed clothes on the bus, popped two Valiums, and met the officers waiting for me behind the venue. They handcuffed me, put me in a squad car, and started driving me down to the station.

We pulled out of the parking lot, alongside some fans exiting the venue. The cruiser circled by the coffee shop and from the backseat I looked up at its marquee, which had been changed. TALLAHASSEE PUNKS: 1, AGAINST ME: 0.

I woke up to find my mugshot plastered all over the front pages of music websites along with my arrest report for battery. "Hair: Brown. Identifying marks: Tattoos all over. Sex: M."

There were two messages waiting for me, one from my manager with a list of legal defense options and the other from the Boss, Springsteen himself. Bruce had praised our band in the press and come out to see us play, an always gracious, humble guest, and about as low-key as you can get if you're Bruce Springsteen.

Dear Tom,

Hope all is well. In regards to some of the criticism you say you've been taking for your great album, some real smart guy once said "he who is not busy being born, is busy dying" (Dylan). I still hold that to be true. I can't count the amount of changes I've been through that have pissed off some fans. If you have a long career, not only will that happen over and over again, but it's supposed to. The Clash's second album, *Give 'Em Enough Rope*, was produced by Sandy Pearlman, high production values, hard guitars, and received some similar criticism from "the faithful." Who remembers that now besides old guys like me? Nobody. All they remember is the Clash went on to be one of the most important bands we'd ever seen. It just comes with the turf. If you're not reaching out beyond the audience you have to the greater audience you might have, you'll never find out what your band is truly capable of, what it's worth, and how much meaning you can bring into your fans' lives. If you act honorably, which means writing well, performing like it's the only thing that matters on a nightly basis, and giving the best of yourself to pull out the best in your audience, you've done your job. Then you let the chips fall where they may. Protect your heart, your art, your band, your friendships, then CHARGE ON, BROTHER, CHARGE ON! I'll be catching up with you along the way. Come out and see us any time.

Bruce Springsteen

I felt humiliated in front of Heather. I had let my band down. I had let Bruce down, too.

Afterward, my legal charges hung above me like a dark cloud that followed me to every city we went to. In an effort to strengthen my case, my attorney asked me to provide a portfolio of press clippings about the band to prove that I was famous. None of them were helpful, though, because they all mentioned my battery on an officer when I was a teenager. There was even one article from a few years prior where I told a journalist that I liked fighting. I have no idea what made me say that. I hated fighting. I'd never even won a fight, and had a long history of getting my ass kicked. I pointed him to the issue of *Maximum Rocknroll* that encouraged people to attack me so that the court would understand the aggression I was constantly faced with.

The stress drove me further and further down a hole of alcohol and cocaine. Binges turned into benders that lasted for months. It became impossible not to drink before shows, usually at least half a bottle of Jameson. If I wasn't drunk, all I could think about were the charges against me. The stakes were high, and I was blowing it.

Touring in support of *New Wave* felt like a fight to the death that we weren't winning. We were on the road all year, playing tours that were financially disastrous and destroying the band's relationship.

A strange dynamic had developed within the band that no one could really explain. When three of us were together, our relationship was fine. But with all four of us, we'd always end up at each other's throats. If our significant others were with us, it threw gas onto the fire. Andrew and I in particular had a difficult time communicating. Sometimes entire days would go by on tour without us talking. We wouldn't even make eye contact when we passed each other in the venues. My paranoia would lead me to run through dark scenarios in my head, imagining what he was thinking about me, and I'm sure he was doing the same.

It all came to a head one night in Rhode Island, on a stretch where Andrew and I hadn't spoken in over three days. I couldn't remember ever feeling that unhappy on a tour. Two songs into our set at Lupo's Heartbreak Hotel, I walked over to his side of the stage and shouted in his ear over the feedback, "I like this deal we have worked out between us. You don't talk to me unless I talk to you first, and I won't talk to you unless you talk to me first. That way, we'll never have to talk again."

I wanted to provoke a reaction out of him, and I got it. He punched me square in the chest, sending me back a few feet. "Go fuck yourself, man!" he shouted. "I quit, how about that?"

We rushed through the rest of our set and I stormed off stage. The crowd was chanting for an encore, but I pushed my way through everyone to the backstage exit. I headed to the bus and grabbed my bags. My plan was to split—stay at a hotel and work out a flight in the morning. Halfway to leaving, I stopped, turned around, and headed back into the venue, where I could still hear the crowd cheering for us.

"You got anything else you want to say?" Andrew asked when I came back in. He didn't wait for me to give an answer, not that I had one worth a damn. He laid into me, told me he was sick of my shit, that I manipulated everyone, and that he hated being in a band with me.

"You can't quit," I pleaded.

"Why not?"

I stood in silence because I could think of no reason other than that the band was all I had. But I couldn't bring myself to say that. I couldn't reveal how lonely I truly was.

I asked Warren and James if they wanted to quit too. James said no. Warren, in his typical passive-aggressive way, said, "It seems like that's what happening right now."

The crowd was still out there, still chanting for that encore, so we agreed to put everything aside for a few minutes and give it to them. We marched back on stage, picked up our instruments, and as we started the intro to "We Laugh at Danger..." the entire place erupted. The long wait for our return built up an excitement in the crowd. Bodies went flying in a blur of fists and singing faces.

Sometimes being in a band is a lot like being in a sexual relationship. If you don't communicate properly, you're destined for explosive fights, but the makeup sex will be incredible. Despite our differences, I really loved Andrew. He and I caught eyes mid-song as a thousand people jumped up and down and sang along.

"This is why you can't quit!" I shouted to him. He smiled at me, and I smirked back.

November 2, 2007--Asbury Park, NJ

Tomorrow we're headlining the Saints and
Sinners Festival. Ticket sales are low. The
promoter overpaid for us and he's losing
his ass. There's mythology surrounding
the area here, the convention center is
cool because it's forever tied to Springsteen but it sounds like shit playing there

unless you're actually Springsteen. This is
our schedule for the day:

   8:00 AM--Bus Arrives at Venue

   8:45 AM--Crew Lobby Call

   9:00 AM--Load In

   10:15 AM--Band Lobby call

   10:30 AM--Sound Check

   12:30 PM to 1:30 PM--Radio interview with
WHTG

   2:00 PM to 5:00 PM--Photo shoot for *Magnet Magazine*

   6:30 PM--Interview with XM Radio

   7:00 PM--Interview with WSOU

   7:30 PM--Interview with the Cleveland *Scene*

   10:30 PM--Set Time

We can't say no to anything. Every show
and every interview, everything offered,
we agree to.

I've passed the point of feeling tired.
I have a headache. My eyes hurt. No real
sleep on the plane. Nothing vegan on the
hotel lobby restaurant menu that I can eat.

November 10, 2007--Orlando, FL

You can't help but feel a little ridiculous being in a punk band that's playing
at the House Of Blues in Downtown Disney
in Orlando, Florida. The stage is walking
distance from Pleasure Island for fuck's
sake. Outside of the venue, families amble

along, pushing strollers carrying whiny
brats wearing Mickey Mouse ears on their
heads while high on sugar and cartoon fan-
tasies. The location trivializes anything
you have to say on stage. What a joke we
are and the audience knows it.

You don't see all the people in the
room who are singing along with their
fists pumping in the air. You just see
the people in the room who aren't singing
along. You see the people leaving through
the ones who stay.

Punks yell "fuck *New Wave*!" in between
every song we play. They hate our new
album. I'm a fool and I let it get to me.
I can't focus and I play horribly. The set
feels like it's never going to end. I'd
like to think that wasn't me up on stage
tonight but it was.

This is the first time I've ever really
hated being on tour. I want to go back to
the bus and crawl into my bunk and die.
I want my heart to stop beating. The band
and crew can find me blue-faced and cold
to the touch in the morning.

November 16, 2007

Andrew starts off the conversation apologizing. I apologize to Andrew in return.
Warren tells me how much he doesn't like

me. "I like you when you make an effort."
Warren tells me this band isn't his whole
life, it's just part of his life. He tells
me that if the band broke up today he
wouldn't die. I tell Warren that if the
band were to break up today that I would
feel like I was dying. Warren wants to
tour less and spend more time with his
"loved ones." He makes a point in empha-
sizing "loved ones" a couple times when
talking. He is telling me that I am not
one of his "loved ones." I get it.

I tell Warren that I'm just blown away
that he's surprised by our hectic schedule right now and that if he didn't want
to tour he shouldn't have signed a fucking million-dollar major label record deal.
You don't get the money for free. You have
to work for it. Warren tells me we aren't
very inspiring right now. I make the argument that this is the most inspiring we've
ever been. It may be ugly but who's to say
ugliness isn't inspiring? We're absolutely
pushed to our limits. We're climbing Ever-
est. Frostbite has set in. This journey will
surely cost limbs. We've run out of food
and we're turning to cannibalism. No one
gets to leave with their sanity intact. That
wouldn't be fair. There's a whole big world
full of sensible balanced people, what's so
goddamn inspiring about any of them?

November 20, 2007--Cleveland, OH

The past two days have taken years
off of my life. I've talked to a million
people--friends I wish I could talk to
more, journalists I feel stupid for talking to, and label suits I never want to
talk to again. If the past couple of days
were made into a cartoon flip book, it
would be one of me progressively fading.

We have a rule about not playing shows
on Monday nights but here we are playing a
show on a Monday night. No one is paying
attention to what we're agreeing to anymore. Interviews all day long today, radio
station performance, meet and greet with
contest winners, then finally after all
that, we play a show.

I worry. I worry that I'm losing my
hair. I worry that I'm getting fat. I worry
that I'm going to have a cocaine-induced
stroke and spend the rest of my life using
my diminished brain capacity to think
about how I had it all and then I threw
it away. I worry that I'm going to get
arrested and convicted of a crime and then
sentenced to years in jail. I worry that
it will be a sentence just long enough to
leave me with some life left when I get
out but forever damaged, emotionally dead.
I worry that I am too self-centered and
egotistical, arrogant and vain. I worry.

We all joked as we headed up on stage tonight that we should get matching shovel tattoos. We've been digging deep.

I've ignored a call from my father everyday since my birthday.

November 22, 2007--Chicago, IL

Just woke up from a dream. Andrew's wife and I are lying side by side on our backs on the floor of the otherwise empty tour bus. I have female genitalia, a detail which I am ecstatic about.

Verité slides her hand down into her pants and starts pleasuring herself. I do the same. She tells me how happy she is for me and how glad she is that we can relate to each other in this way. She turns and moves in to kiss me and her face freezes in time. She is suddenly grotesque and unbeautiful. The thought of my wife enters my head and I pull away. I rise to my feet and her face melts into a look of embarrassment and rejection.

In the dream, Andrew and the rest of the band and crew come crowding back into the bus. We act natural, like nothing was going on.

"I'm sorry," I silently mouth to Verité. Dream ends.

I've taken three shots of Scotch in an attempt to put myself back to sleep. It only makes me want another shot of Scotch. I don't even like Scotch.

December 4, 2007--Boston, MA

The Tampa radio station festival show was terrible, absolutely awful. We didn't fit on the radio rock bill. It wasn't our scene of bands. None of us wanted to be there.

"I feel like a whore," Andrew said after the set.

I hated looking out while playing and seeing the tops of Army recruitment tents. I hate being a part of events like this. I hate not saying anything against it from stage. I want to tell every kid here to go tear those fucking Army tents down, for-get college, drop out of high school, get drunk, get high, get smart, get pissed, get even. I feel like a sellout.

We are *Rolling Stone*'s #9 album of the year, #5 in *Blender*, and #1 in *SPIN*. But when a former fan writes to me, saying, "Your old fans are dropping like flies. I hope this whole thing implodes in your faces," it crushes me.

December 10, 2007--San Diego, CA

We walked off stage to a mix of boos
and applause.

Not only were there military recruit-
ers present at the San Diego radio station
show, the whole event was sponsored by the
Marine Corps. Neither management nor the
label told us this information when talking us into playing these events. I found
out when I heard the radio DJ introducing us over the PA and thanking the show's
sponsors. I don't want to play shows for
the war machine. This was embarrassing.

My resentment grew and grew until I
could take it no more. During the last
song, I told the crowd that had we known
that the Marines were a sponsor we would
not have agreed to play. I told them that
isn't what our band is about and that
we're against the U.S. military-industrial
complex. I asked the audience not to buy
our merchandise and I apologized for being
there. I feel like a chump for having
played the show and I feel like a chump
for having said anything.

I hate that my hands shake when I'm
angry.

———

You can high-five me in the elevator," my lawyer whispered as
we walked out of the office. I should have been happy, but I was

so angry with myself. The judge in my case agreed to withhold adjudication after I apologized and accepted that I was at fault. It didn't hurt that the plaintiff in the case had been arrested for armed robbery a couple weeks after the coffee shop incident. We would not go to court and no conviction would appear on my criminal record, as long as I paid a fine and fulfilled community service.

What a stupid mistake. A stupid, $35,000 mistake. Still, it was the day before my 27th birthday and, considering how many musicians like Kurt Cobain, Janis Joplin, Jim Morrison, and Jimi Hendrix all met their demise at that age, I figured things could be worse. I was relieved to put it past me and move on. No longer did I have to walk around with the burden of legal uncertainty. I could just exist.

For all our hard work over a year that nearly tore us apart, *New Wave* charted higher and sold more copies in the first week than all of our previous records. We played on *Letterman, Leno, Conan,* and *Kimmel.* The mainstream music press showered the album with critical praise, drawing comparisons to "this generation's Clash," and the CD ended up selling 100,000 copies worldwide. This was a monumental accomplishment for the band, but a tremendous disappointment for the label because it didn't go gold. The label didn't care about critical acclaim. They wanted sales figures, and 100,000 copies meant nothing to them. They wanted half a million, at least, and really wanted a million. It felt like all of our efforts had come up short.

I was asked in an end-of-the-year interview, "When is the breaking point? How much is too much?" Although I didn't say so, I felt that I'd found that breaking point and was ready for a vacation.

Heather and I did a fair job of keeping secret the fact that we were already married. We had always planned on having an actual wedding ceremony at the end of the year. I wanted that experience for us because it was my second marriage. I wanted this time to be different. Maybe with a real ceremony, the commitment would actually mean something. I wanted to have a first dance together and feed each other wedding cake. I wanted to get married for the last time.

In December, we headed back to South Beach once again for a proper wedding at the National Hotel, right down the street from the courthouse where we had our private ceremony earlier that year. I wore a tuxedo custom-tailored to fit me, and Heather wore a black gown. We kept it intimate, around 100 guests, mostly family, both blood and band family.

The wedding was the first time in almost 20 years that my mother and father had been in the same room. I had to make sure they were seated far apart from each other at all times. Not only did I have their tables at opposite ends of the room during the reception, but their seats had their backs to each other. Though the setting was intimate, they avoided each other the whole time.

All of my band came to the wedding and all of Alkaline Trio showed up for Heather. Even Nolan made the trip, although Matt Skiba told him he couldn't come to the wedding after starting a fistfight at the bar the night before.

Heather and I left for our honeymoon shortly after, spending Christmas and New Year's in Rome, just the two of us. I should have bought first-class plane tickets, but everything else about the trip was a five-star experience, starting with a limousine driver waiting for us at the Leonardo da Vinci Airport arrival gate, holding a sign reading our now-shared name, "Gabel."

We spent two weeks taking in the amazing Italian sights—the Basilica, the Pantheon, the Sistine Chapel, the Capuchin Crypts, but mostly just sitting outside of cafés in the Campo Di Fiori, drinking espresso in the mornings, wine at night, and eating all the penne arrabiata we could. I hadn't had a cigarette in over five years, but allowed myself to smoke all I wanted there. When in Rome, right?

We stuck our hands in La Bocca della Verità, as is the custom, and I pretended it bit mine off. We ice skated along the banks of the Fiume Tevere, in front of the Castel Sant'Angelo, bought masterpieces off of street painters while stumbling drunk along the Via Del Corso, and paid a euro for the basement tour of the Profondo Rosso Museum of Horrors. We never made it to the Villa Borghese, though.

There was a New Year's Eve party on the roof of our hotel, next door to the Colosseum, with all the guests and staff popping bottles of champagne and dancing. I don't remember the countdown or kiss, and ended the night in typical New Year's fashion, gripping porcelain tight and heaving all my guts up. As I laid on the cold tile of the bathroom floor, leaving 2007 a spinning mess behind me, I had the feeling that I was at a turning point. I just didn't know in which direction I was turning.

6. DON'T ABANDON ME

There were 10,000 people in front of us and a giant black banner hanging behind us, decorated with the cover of *New Wave*. No band name, just the face of the snarling panther.

Against Me! kicked off 2008 on a stadium tour opening for Foo Fighters. We had to ask Sire for over $30,000 in tour support because the gig paid practically nothing. We had turned down a tour opening for Linkin Park that would have actually made us money, just to go out with the Foos. Linkin Park had cash, but Foo Fighters had credibility. We took the opportunity hoping it would turn a whole new audience on to us, but we didn't do much to help ourselves there.

We would walk out onto the gigantic stage every night, pick up our instruments, and start playing. No "hello," no "we're Against Me!," not a word, just a four-count into the first song and then straight through the set without break. I'd look out into the audience from the stage and see faces in the front row glued to their phones. I could sense the disinterest, like if we didn't care to tell them who we were, then why should they care to find out? Still, we did pick up some fans each night, those who walked away wondering, "Who was that band in black?" and actually bothered to investigate.

I didn't want to talk on stage for a few reasons. For one, every time I opened my mouth, all I could hear was a voice that sounded too close to my father's blasting through a huge PA system. But also because it had been disillusioning to learn over the years that bands that I'd loved would say the same exact thing to their audiences every night. Same words, same jokes, same banter. All part of the act. I didn't want to turn into that. I wasn't a politician, and I wasn't a comedian. I wasn't trying to sell people anything, save for maybe a few records and T-shirts. And on top of all that, I never really knew what to say anyway.

Arena and stadium touring was a completely new experience. I was so blown away by the size of the operation. I've always thought it was important to take the time to know the people you're on tour with, at least catch their names and say hey around the venue. This was impossible in this setting. The scale of the operation was just damn remarkable—dozens of semi trucks and their drivers, crew people to load them, multiple stage techs for each band member, not just singular sound engineers and lighting designers, but whole teams for each function, not to mention the tour buses and drivers to carry all these souls. There was no way you could expect to even see the faces of all the people traveling with this circus, and I quickly gave up. My favorite thing to do on this tour was to climb to a high vantage point in the arena before and after each show and just watch everyone work to build or tear down the stage. Truly impressive.

Even though there were so many people zipping past us at all times, the experience was extremely isolating. It's an odd thing to feel so alone surrounded by that many people. When you're the opening band on a tour like that, you have endless free time.

You wake up in some underground parking garage in a sports arena outside of town. Aside from whatever press obligations you have, which take place somewhere in the venue most often, you have limited responsibilities. Breakfast, lunch, and dinner are prepared and waiting for you at the designated times so you don't have to worry about that.

Your backstage room is the visiting team's locker room. (The headliner gets the home team's locker room.) Black curtains are draped over the lockers, and a couple couches or chairs are thrown in, as well as a folding table covered with snacks and beverages, cold cuts, veggies, and Clif Bars. I could never eat another Clif Bar again and die happy.

As the opener, there's no sound check. If you sleep until noon, that's an eight-hour window of time to kill before the show. All that waiting for a 30-minute set, and then another eight or 10 hours until bus call, just sitting there backstage. Same schedule, day after day. This particular tour was three months long. This is why bands drink and do drugs, and why they're addicted to smartphones and computers. Touring is lonely and monotonous and often boring.

The Foo Fighters were more than welcoming to us, though. It's reasonable to expect a band of their size to be completely cut off from the openers, and I wouldn't have been surprised if we had gone the whole three months without even meeting any of them. But I'll never forget that first day of tour, turning a corner in the venue to see Dave Grohl's big smiling face and outstretched hand coming in to shake mine, quickly striding toward me...

"Hey, I'm Dave!"

Inside, I was screaming, *Of course you are! You played in fucking Nirvana. There isn't a person out there who owns a guitar pick or a drumstick who doesn't know your name.* But instead I just returned the introduction and nervously mumbled something about being grateful to be on board.

Night after night, I watched in awe as Dave and the rest of the band held the massive crowds in the palms of their hands like the well-oiled machine they are. I developed a new appreciation for this world, contrary to what the DIY punk scene had instilled in me. That's the lie of punk. Sure, you can play a 20-minute set through a barely audible PA and make the kids in the basement go off and tell yourself it's the noble path, but can you do what Dave Grohl and his band do? Can you hold the attention of thousands for almost three hours? Or is it easier just to dismiss that kind of rock and roll as too corporate and lacking artistic merit? I realized how inadequate I was as a performing artist. I was so inspired by this deficiency that I wanted to learn from the experience and grow from it.

I'm not sure the rest of the band took the tour as a learning experience. Their wives and girlfriends came along with us for stretches, and they stayed with them most of the time, while I avoided everyone. We were still cold and distant from each other, and arena touring gives you the space to do that. If they were in the dressing room backstage, I would stay on the bus. If they were on the bus, I'd be in the dressing room. The only time we really spent together was right before our set.

Our last show of the tour was at the iconic Wembley Arena in London to a crowd of 80,000 people, every single one of them there to see the Foo Fighters, not us. Andrew made a comment before the set: "Well, at least we made it to Wembley."

"I'm not counting it until we come back as the headliner," I responded. I wanted to be the ones people came to see, and I wasn't going to rest until the vision was realized. I felt at odds with the ambition of the rest of my band. I wanted them to see the vision, too.

We were so close, right there on the precipice, playing in front of the largest audiences of our career, but we weren't con- necting with the crowds because we weren't connecting with each other. The wide open spaces of arena touring had done nothing to improve band communications. I still hated everyone and everyone still hated me. Opportunities kept coming in and we kept saying yes to them; there was no stopping. We needed a sacrifice, someone or something to hold accountable for our lack of functionality so we could continue on as we'd always done. Desperate for a scapegoat, we did something we'd been talking about doing for ages. We fired our manager.

He had babysat us through the years up until this point, dealing with all my bullshit, and was still continuing to grow the band. Despite my arrest and legal woes, we had just had the most successful year of the band's history. A week after playing our highest paying gig to date, a $75,000 paycheck for one Southern Comfort–sponsored free show in Atlanta that the manager organized, we dropped the axe. Coming to a unanimous decision on this move gave the four of us a sense of solidarity we hadn't experienced in a long time, but our excitement quickly dwindled when we actually had to let him go and realized we were faced with the question: What next? Of course, we went ahead and fired the lawyer, too, while we were at it, because why not clean house and start fresh?

Managerless, we headed back out on the Warped Tour, which was a bleak, tiring version of what we remembered from two years back. None of the bands we had befriended were back this time around, and gone was our preferential treatment. What once felt like punk rock summer camp was now nothing but an arduous blur of sunscreen, sweat, and dirt.

"What the hell are you all doing back on this tour?" Stephen Christian of the band Anberlin asked me, puzzled upon seeing us on the first day. "You all had *Spin*'s #1 album, and you agreed to do the Warped Tour again? Why?"

It wasn't a rhetorical question, but I pretended it was because I didn't have a good answer. I wasn't sure who our audience even was anymore. We had lost credibility in the DIY punk scene by doing the Warped Tour the first time around, and now by being back on the tour, we were losing the credibility with the hip media outlets we had worked so hard to gain traction with.

It was the end of George W. Bush's presidency, and the economy was so fucked that we were budgeting $20,000 just for gas. We also made the mistake of agreeing to do daily meet-and-greet signings, which made us hate each other even more. Two hours after every set posing for pictures in 100-degree heat in the parking lots of America will do that to you.

When the tour went to L.A., we interviewed a series of potential new managers, each one more clueless about us than the last. One of them, Axl Rose's former manager, told me over dinner that we should be taking advantage of the opportunity to get paid by the Army for performing for troops overseas. He stroked our egos, telling us we were the greatest band in the world. I responded by asking him to name our albums. He couldn't come up with a single one besides *New Wave*. "That kind of knowledge isn't really important in this business," he told me.

Finally, after being worn down by a seemingly endless line of manager meetings like this, we impulsively hired the first one who could hold a reasonably enjoyable conversation with us, Ian Montone. It was his roster of bands that really sold me— the White Stripes, M.I.A., and the Shins, among others. These were the type of bands we wanted to be associated with, successful bands that sold concert tickets and albums, and got songs placed in movies. Bands that were galaxies away from the world of Warped Tour.

The high we all felt from this big change was immediately deflated by a call from our label A&R. "What the fuck did you just do?!" he snarled at me with an ice-cold tone. He told me that he absolutely refused to work with Ian, that Ian had "fucked him over on a deep and personal level," but wouldn't explain how. It was a difficult position to be put in. Our whole decision suddenly became a mess of confusion, and it was hard to separate fear from logic. I was so sick of thinking about managers.

Writing songs at a furious pace, I was chomping at the bit to get back in the studio. I had been bringing songs to the band all summer, but the reaction from them was lukewarm at best. The rest of the band was ultimately on board, but Warren said he just "didn't know how to come up with a drum beat for some songs," which I found unacceptable. I bought a drum machine and set up a recording time, entering the studio prepared to play all of the instruments myself along with my new battery-operated beat-making friend. The label wanted me to release it as an EP under the name Against Me! because it would sell more copies, but I insisted on releasing it under my own name as a solo effort. It ended up being called Tom Gabel's *Heart Burns*. This did nothing for inner-band relations, and the label did nothing to promote it. We were imploding, and we would have been done for good had I not gotten the phone call.

I was on my way out the door, heading to dinner in Naples with my wife and mother, when Andrew called in a panic to warn me.

"If someone you don't know comes knocking at your door, do not answer! I just got fucking served with papers from Sarig. They're going to serve all of us!"

Our former manager was suing us for $1.24 million. My stomach started to churn with anxiety and my eyelid wouldn't stop twitching. $1.24 million. It was more money than the four of us would have had if we sold everything we owned. I hadn't even been out of legal trouble for a year, and again I was being dragged back into the system.

Being sued feels like an act of violence being committed on your very existence. You are completely defenseless against it.

October 9, 2008--Washington DC

Ian MacKaye was at our Black Cat show
tonight. The whole time we were playing, I
felt conscious of his presence and what a
sellout I am.

The entertainment lawyer--the lawyer who
negotiated our major label deal and who we
fired along with the manager--is withholding files we need for the lawsuit, saying
that we owe him $2,500. We paid him $70k
for one contract and now he's hard-balling
us for $2,500. What a shitbag weasel.

We've never even met the lawyer defend-
ing us in the lawsuit. He's just some
voice on the other end of a conference
call, a name attached to emails, and the
name we're writing checks out to. His
first course of action has been to ask for
an extension of time from the judge. He
also filed for a dismissal based on there
being no contract between us and the manager, but it will be months before we hear
back on that. This lawsuit is going to
take years to play out.

I feel no motivation to write in my
journal, to write lyrics, to write songs.
I'm not sure when, if ever, during the
day I'm present. It all seems pointless,
like a fight I can't possibly win, my only
choice is to give in. Someone will always
own you. I wonder if it's not too late to
explore a different career. I wonder if I

would be happier with a different vocation.
I could go back to school. Journalism? Law?
Anything besides music. Is it too late?

My afternoon phone interview with the
LA Times had a political slant to it. The
journalist asked really esoteric, abstract
questions about our music. I hate interviews. They feel like homework and I'm just
trying to guess the right answers so the
journalist will write an article that will
help us sell records.

"What purpose do you think music serves
in protest movements?" I don't fucking
care. I'm a sellout. Why are you asking
me? I can't answer the question honestly
so I make up some meaningless garbage.

More depressed than ever. Considering
suicide.

October 22, 2008--SLC, Utah--8:47 PM

First and foremost, I am glad that we
are all unharmed, alive.

Everyone was asleep when it happened.
I woke up to the sound of screaming, the
sensation of spinning, the sound of crashing inside and outside of the bus. My eyes
opened to the blackness. I immediately
pressed my hands and feet onto the roof of
my bunk as hard as I could, bracing for
what I did not know.

When we stopped, our bus driver started calling out names one by one to make sure everyone was okay. I didn't want to wake up, moments before I was so deeply asleep. I was annoyed. It wasn't until I got off my bunk that I realized how completely un-level to the ground the bus was, we were almost completely on our side. The contents of the bus were thrown everywhere up and down the hallway--luggage, food, DVDs, video games, broken glass.

Looking out the front window of the bus, I saw that our trailer was laying on its side and our bus driver was out there try-ing to quickly push our gear, which was strewn all along the highway, to the side of the road. I sleep fully dressed on the bus just in case something like this happens, so I don't have to search for my clothes.

The eastbound lanes of the highway, where most of the gear was laying, was closed down. The westbound lane was not and as we all scrambled to push gear to the side of the road. A semi-truck hit the same patch of ice we had, spun out of control, narrowly missing our bus, and landed in the median just behind it. A couple rescue vehicles showed up and we were advised not to get back into the bus. It was freezing cold. We were offered two blankets to share amongst the ten of us.

The tour manager caught a ride into Rawlins, Wyoming, which was about 50 miles

```
away where he rented a U-Haul truck. We
waited on the side of the road for him to
come back so we could load the U-Haul with
our battered, broken gear. Andrew and I
drove the U-Haul to SLC, the bus followed
behind us. We had to cancel the show.
```

With no fanfare or acknowledgement, another year of touring came to an end for Against Me!. We had spent 245 days on tour in 2008. I felt like I'd finally run out of road, my career was over. I was hated, uninteresting, and outdated.

We all showed up to our practice space in Gainesville on the last day of the year, having not seen each other since our last tour had ended weeks ago. We'd cancelled our France run in December, knowing it wasn't going to make us any money, and with the lawsuit hanging over our heads, none of us were interested in taking the financial hit.

No one talked at first. We just set up our instruments in silence. For a few minutes, we all sat in a circle, looking at each other as our amps hummed behind us. Warren opened it up. He said that he thought the band was diseased, that it had a sickness, and that he could never envision himself being excited about playing music with the three of us again. I knew what he meant. He meant that *I* was diseased, and that he could never see himself being excited about playing music with *me* again. "Yeah, well, right back at you, buddy," I thought. "I might be a shitty person, but you have terrible meter."

Warren and I went back and forth, airing our grievances and venting repressed hatred of one another. Andrew made futile attempts at maintaining some middle ground between us, and James, as usual, barely said anything at all. If he had opinions, he sure did a hell of a job of keeping them to himself.

Then, after we had spent almost an hour talking about how

we couldn't stand to play music together anymore, we picked up our instruments and started working on a new song. What else could we do? We were being sued for over a million dollars. This was the only way to keep money coming in to afford the increasingly expensive legal bills we were being slammed with. We all hated each other, but we hated the manager more. At least we were united in that.

Plus, we were contractually obligated to deliver another album to Sire. More accurately, and ironically thanks to the manager and lawyer, Sire was contractually obligated to release one more album by us. We had what was called a "two firm deal," meaning no matter how badly the first album did, on top of the million dollars they had already given us, they still had to give us another $500,000 to record a follow-up. Butch had already asked if we would do another album with him.

Against Me! felt less like a band and more like a prison sentence we were all handed with no foreseeable release date. Our only chance of escaping the straits we were in was for me to write our most successful album to date.

So this was my plan. I knew we had the war fund of label cash, and I wanted to fight. Fuck Warren, fuck Andrew, and fuck James, I thought. I had already accepted that I was in it on my own, and no one else was going to contribute creatively. The songwriting was all on me.

I was determined to do it. Not confident, but determined. I wrote my New Year's resolution on the wall before shutting the lights: "Write a hit fucking record."

I took the long way home from practice that night, through the coastal roads of Saint Augustine, loaded up on rage and Adderall, and desperate for inspiration. I hung a right onto King Street, driving past the coral towers of Flagler College and the old slave market, an open-air pavilion where Africans were once traded and sold. Not far ahead was a beach that housed shoreline race riots in the 1960s as well as the jail that famously held Martin Luther King Jr. for a night in June of 1964 after his sole Florida arrest. His crime: daring to eat at a restaurant in the Monson Motor Lodge.

Just before midnight hit, and brought with it another year of uncertainty, I headed north on San Marco Avenue, stopping in front of the Mission of Nombre De Dios and La Leche Shrine. To the right, an anti-abortion display of four thousand crosses, one for every fetus aborted every day in America, arranged neatly in front of the world's tallest cross, which stood 208 feet high, erected to mark the site where Christianity first landed in America in 1565.

I looked upon my city for an epiphany, but all I saw around me were monuments to its mistakes and reminders of the disgrace buried deep within its soil. White crosses on the church lawn—I wanted to smash them all.

7. WHITE CROSSES

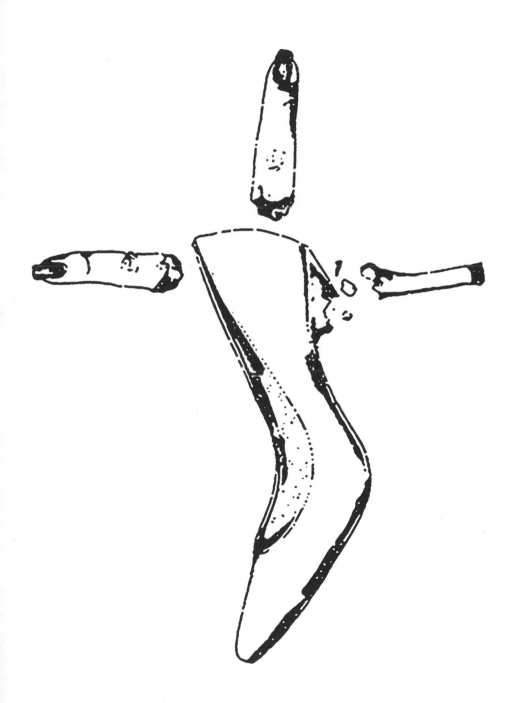

We took a third test just to be sure. Another blue line, another positive result. Heather was pregnant. It took me hours just to comprehend the implications behind this information. Somewhere in the dark, our baby was forming, coming to life, a son or daughter. Heather was going to be a mother. I was going to be a father.

My instinct was to rush out and buy a crib, call family and friends, and start celebrating. But I knew I was getting ahead of myself. One thing at a time. Heather scheduled a doctor's appointment for the next morning to get some official word before telling our parents. We'd wait the recommended three months before telling friends.

This wasn't a surprise pregnancy. We had been trying to have a baby. Heather had come off of birth control over the summer and started taking prenatal vitamins, which we had been busted for after the band discovered them in the tour bus fridge that past summer on Warped Tour. We denied we were trying for it, but there aren't a lot of other reasons to take prenatal vitamins.

The pregnancy was well planned, even, to fit into the time between album touring cycles. Still, the full impact didn't hit me until the doctor told us this was for real. We were going to be responsible for a human life, a little person that we didn't even know yet, a person that shared our DNA and our characteristics. I couldn't even comprehend the magnitude of it all.

It has to be a girl, I thought. *Please let it be a girl. Oh fuck, what if it's a boy?* The possibility of having a boy terrified me, knowing I wouldn't be able to be the proper male role model he would need. Heather didn't want to know ahead of time, insisting it be a surprise, so I'd have to wait. She said if it ended up being a boy, she'd want to name him Tommy. The superstitious wishes I used to make on things like finding a penny heads up or seeing a shooting star turned from "I wish for a platinum selling record" to "I wish for a healthy baby girl." Please, just let it be a girl, and let her be healthy.

Heather's sister was also expecting when we found out, a couple months further along, so she invited Heather to visit for a week in Belgium, where she lived with her husband, a pro basketball player on the European circuit. They were excited to share their pregnancies together. I was excited for the time alone to focus on writing songs. I called off band practice for the week with the intention of hunkering down, just me and my acoustic guitar.

Even with the privacy of Heather being gone, writing was still daunting. Not only did the record need to be good enough to ward off the lawsuit and save the band, but it would now have to produce enough income to support a family. The pressure had doubled. I smoked a bowl of weed that first morning she was gone, sitting there on our blue velvet living room couch, eager to relieve the stress of these thoughts, and then took a hot shower.

When I came out, I wrapped a fresh towel around my waist and went into the bedroom. There were reminders of Heather everywhere. Her perfume sat in a little bottle on her vanity. I picked it up and smelled the tip of it, breathing her in. I sprayed it into the air, stuck my nose into the mist, and inhaled. I held the bottle up to the side of my neck and pushed the button down, feeling the cool, fragrant drops as they landed on me, from my Adam's apple down to my clavicle. I turned my cheek and sprayed the other side as well.

The door to the closet was open. I walked in and turned on the light, all of Heather's beautiful black vintage gowns hanging in front of me. I took down a summer dress and held it in my hands, feeling the delicacy of the material in my fingertips. Almost not realizing what I was doing, I slipped it on over my head. "Tom, no," a voice inside me whispered, but it was a slow surrender, an urge I was powerless to fight. "Well maybe just this one last time," the voice conceded. I stepped into a pair of her high heels. We wore the same size shoes, and they fit perfectly.

What an absolute relief. It felt so good. My shoulders relaxed from the tension of the fight-or-flight state they had been in for years. I later went out and bought a couple of wigs for fun, intent on spending the rest of the week at home as "her." It was enough to just sit in the silence of the house, the fading Florida sun streaming through the cracks in the blinds. I wanted the world, but this would have to suffice. Menial chores like doing the dishes, vacuuming, organizing receipts ahead of tax season—no matter how boring, they were exciting as her. My guitar sat silent in the corner. That wasn't her guitar; that was his. Record label pressures, lawsuit looming, marriage responsibilities, baby on the way—those were his problems. That was his life, not mine.

At the end of my week, I drove to pick up Heather from the airport, checking my face in the rearview mirror at every red light. I had scrubbed my eyes raw making sure all traces of her eyeliner were gone, but it still wasn't enough. I stopped at a drugstore to buy makeup remover, and kept vigorously rubbing my eyelids in the car.

I threw the cleaning wipes, the bag, and the receipt out the window before pulling up to curbside pick-up. The makeup was gone, but I could still feel the guilt drawn on my face. Heather hugged me as she approached the car with her luggage, but I couldn't look her in the eye for fear that she'd know. Seeing Heather snapped me back to the real world. The relief I'd experienced all week was gone, replaced by shame and paranoia.

On the ride back to our place, where I had been meticulous about putting all of Heather's belongings back exactly the way I'd found them before she left, she told me stories about her trip and gave updates on how her body was adapting to the pregnancy. I tried to listen, but I was sweating the whole way home, wondering how I'd let this happen again. I hadn't worn a woman's clothes in almost five years, and I hadn't worn Heather's clothes ever. I'd slipped up and relapsed. I didn't understand why it was suddenly back, or how it had found me.

Wasn't it all behind me?

While the news of Heather's pregnancy continued to hit me like waves over the following weeks, it turned out that Warren had some big news of his own. He was opening up a Mexican restaurant in Gainesville. He casually told us all out of the blue one morning as we were in the first week of a two-week tour of the Southeast, still nursing hangovers from the night before. He even offered the rest of the band the opportunity to be investors. I was at a complete loss for words. We were being sued, working our asses off to save the band from complete bankruptcy, and he was opening a fucking restaurant?

I later pulled James and Andrew aside and told them I wanted
Warren gone. They didn't disagree. I had already made a couple of calls to line up potential drummers and arranged some
tryouts. I hoped that adding new blood to our chemistry and
ditching the weakest musical link for a better player would give
us that extra push needed for a hit. We conspired to break the
news to him before the end of tour.

All I could think about that whole tour, besides how much
I hated Warren, was how badly I was dying to express my femininity. Everywhere I looked were reminders. I would glance out
into our audience while we played and my eyes would fix on
an attractive woman and keep finding their way back to her
throughout the set—not because I wanted to fuck her like rock
stars are supposed to do, but because I wished I was as pretty as
her, and because of how much I wished her body was my own. I
could almost live it like it was real—close my eyes and I was her,
long hair brushing against my exposed shoulders as I danced in
a trance. Then we'd play a new song, and someone would yell
out "sellout!" or hold up a sign that said YOU FAILED US above an
anarchy symbol, and I'd stumble through the rest of the song,
tripping up on lyrics and tripping over patch cords. I'd scurry to
my amplifier to down another chug from the glass of Jameson
that always rested on top of it.

Three days before the end of tour, I told James and Andrew
it was time. Before the set in Wilmington I grabbed Warren,
told him we needed to talk, and the four of us walked to the
top of a parking garage behind the venue. The sun already
down, and the stadium lights overhead, the scene probably
looked like a drug deal or an execution was about to go down.
We weren't breaking up, we told him; we just didn't want to play
with him anymore. Warren took it in stride. I'm sure he must
have felt ganged-up on and I can't imagine that feeling, when
three in the family decide to eat the fourth. He said he'd still

do the rest of the tour, and we told him he could tell everyone he'd quit.

The next night in Athens at Tasty World was a riot. I'm not sure we had ever played better as a band, but I spoiled the memory of it by getting good and drunk afterward and becoming verbally abusive toward Warren in the hallway of our hotel. I told him what I felt and then some, told him to fuck off. I blinked and the hallways were empty. Everyone was gone. I couldn't remember what room I was in, and didn't have my key even if I could.

I had to piss so badly that I did so right there in a stairwell. I was drunk enough that it seemed logical, even courteous, to piss on the walls as opposed to pissing directly onto the carpet. I thought the housekeeping staff would thank me for this act of thoughtfulness. I drenched the wall and the floor with my piss, collapsed into the puddle, and passed out. I woke up in my room the next morning and didn't know how I'd gotten there. I never saw this, but my mom once told me that my dad used to piss on the walls of our house when I was a kid. He'd come home from the field drunk, get angry, and start pissing. I guess I shared that with him.

I hated myself for getting drunk, not just because I was turning into my father, but because I was already failing at being a father myself. Since Heather stopped partying for the nine months of her pregnancy, giving up weed and alcohol, I wanted to match her sobriety to show her how committed I was. I tried to give it all up to be right there with her. I wanted to read all the baby books she'd read. But I couldn't even get through the first few weeks. I also felt guilty for failing Heather by giving into my dysphoria. That made me get depressed and drink more. I was caught in a perpetual cycle of self-loathing.

Before we took the stage on the last night of tour in Columbia, South Carolina, at the New Brookland Tavern, Warren asked if we could all talk. He told us that he thought we'd made the right decision. He said that he realized a lot of his actions over the last year, though unintentional, were indicative of his not being fully invested in the band.

I fought back tears through the last half of our set that night. I kept looking over the drums and seeing the bearded face that had sat reliably behind me for almost a decade, keeping the beat, however imperfect. We closed with "We Laugh at Danger (And Break All the Rules)," a song Warren and I wrote for *Reinventing Axl Rose* back in 2001, a time when everything seemed so much simpler and easier. We played it together one last time, and I walked off stage, exited through the back of the building, and found a quiet alley where I could be alone. I dropped to my knees and cried. The tears weren't just for Warren leaving; they were for how fucked up everything had gotten. For all of our problems as a band, I had honestly wanted the four of us to succeed together. I had believed in the dream.

After pulling myself together, I went back into the bar, ordered a round of shots for the closest bodies to me, and proceeded to drink until I blacked out. I woke up on the back bench of the van just as we were pulling up to my house. I grabbed my bag and jumped out without saying goodbye.

March 13, 2009--Saint Augustine, FL

Heather and I had just sat down to breakfast when Andrew called to tell me the news. C.C. was dead. She had an argument with her drug-dealer boyfriend. He shot her in the back of the head, tried to hide her body in a closet. He showed up at

a friend's house covered in her blood. They
had called the cops. He had been arrested
and charged with her murder.

At the funeral, C.C.'s mom approached me
and asked if I still had the tattoo of her
daughter's name on the back of my leg. I
was ashamed to tell the truth and say no,
it had been covered. When she next asked
if the song "Thrash Unreal" was about her
daughter, I thought she wanted to hear me
say yes, so I lied and said so. C.C.'s mom
then told me how much the song had hurt and
embarrassed her daughter. They had spoken
about it a couple days before her death. She
made me promise to make it up to her.

It didn't look like C.C. in the casket. It had been a couple years since we
had last seen each other. Since the affair
ended. Her hair was long, she had grown it
out. The makeup made her look tan, which
she most absolutely was not. She would
have hated the dress they put on her.

I felt guilt walking into the room. No
one wanted me there. She was married with
a kid and we once had a relationship. I
didn't know what to say when I saw her
estranged husband. I have never known what
to say to him.

I'm sorry. I loved her, too.

I'm not sure if I remember the past
correctly. Maybe I'm romanticizing things
or leaving out important details. I need
to make good on my promise to C.C.'s mom.

I can't sleep since the funeral. I can't stop thinking about C.C. and the way she was when she was alive. Her corpse was unreal to me. Her sunken eyes. Her sunken cheeks. The bullet hole in the back of her head.

The tattoos on her arms were covered by the long sleeve dress. I'm not sure if she still had "Tom Tom the Atom Bomb" tattooed on her arm but I assume so.

Heather reminded me of C.C. when we first met. That was one of the things that first attracted me to her.

There are so many things that I regret about my relationship with C.C., so many reasons to feel guilt. Because of the shame I associate with vulnerability I am numbing myself completely. Can you hear me right now?

Wrong time, wrong place. Maybe we can be together in the next life.

———

March 21, 2009--Boston, MA--2:04 PM

Somehow the ceiling of room 247 at the Howard Johnson is more stained than the carpet. None of the pictures hang straight on the walls and their placement is suspect, most likely covering holes.

This is my first time at the House of Blues in Boston, since they remodeled the

building. This used to be the Avalon as
well as many different clubs before that.
We've played at the Avalon at least once a
year for the past five. There's not a trace
of the old room left but it still feels
familiar.

You know what to expect when you're
playing a House Of Blues. They're all decorated the same. The sound system is always
good. Backstage is always comfortable. It's
consistent but also feels like you're playing in a Ruby Tuesday restaurant.

The set was okay. Opening solo for the
Pogues. I was too nervous to have fun,
overthinking every action made. None of
the Pogues said so much as a "hello" to
me. They aren't a very friendly bunch.
They don't seem like they're enjoying what
they're doing. Philip Chevron went so far
as to try walking into a locked utility
closet to avoid having to interact with me.

Just off stage right is a small cur-
tained off area. Behind the curtain there
is a table and a chair. On the table is
a tub of ice with a scooper, a stack of
plastic cups, two shot glasses, an ash-
tray, three lighters, two bottles of
gin, a bottle of white wine, a bottle of
tequila, two bottles of whiskey, two bottles of tonic water, a bottle opener and
two stacks of six towels; all for Shane
MacGowan. At various points in the set
he leaves the stage and goes behind the

curtains. The band plays a couple songs
without him and then he comes back out.

I can't imagine what it must be like
to be in a band with him, what it must
be like to watch someone fade so gradually over the years, especially someone so
talented.

March 30, 2009--Saint Augustine, FL

Did I succumb to the inevitable or
give in to the predictable? I have no
self-control. I disgust myself.

For the past week this house has been
my entire world. It has been enough to
exist as her behind these walls, curtains
drawn closed. I sweep, mop, vacuum, dust,
organize, reorganize. I'm terrified to go
outside like this and I'm thankful for
every second of it. The perpetual suck of
life ceases to exist, a moment suspended.
It's like briefly existing in another
dimension, a life that could have been,
bittersweet.

This has to stop after this weekend.
Anything else is to be feared and fought.

I cannot remember the last time I felt
this free. I was ravenous, starved, crazed,
desperate for it.

April 13, 2009--Saint Augustine, FL

Heather and I started the day off with
a big breakfast of tofu scramble, fresh
cut kale from our garden, soy sausage,
toast, and coffee. We watched a VHS collection of Danzig music videos while eating.
"She Rides" has to be one of the greatest
music videos ever made.

We washed the car, worked on the garden, cleaned up around the house and then
headed in for a scheduled ultrasound. Everything looks fine. In the afternoon we
went to the beach, sat in the sand, split
a tomato sandwich.

At 13 weeks, our child can make a fist
and suck its thumb. Bones are solidify-
ing. Soon it will have ribs, intestines
in place, teeth ready to be grown, vocal
cords ready to wail.

I crawl into bed next to Heather and
she sticks me with an elbow, mumbles
"Dammit."

I love you, Heather.

———

April 17, 2009--Asheville, NC

I'm repulsed by the sight of my own
body hair. It's happened to me before.
Comes and goes in waves. Have I lost my
mind? Estranged. Deranged. Perverted.

I'm trying not to drink on this tour,
which isn't easy. Weed helps when the
dysphoria gets to be too much. I need a
crutch.

I need to find a 24-hour Walmart Super
Store or a shopping mall. I need something
feminine to wear. It's the only thing
that's going to keep me sane on this run.

Andrew and Jordan are sitting up front,
singing made-up songs about "butthole
stimulation." Andrew's sense of humor is
reliant on the human asshole, his or other
people's bowel movements, farts, anal sex,
etc. It's harmless but so fucking boring.

Tour has been moving at a quick pace.
Locked into a routine of wake up and
drive, stop for gas, drive some more,
sound-check, find something to eat, wait
for the show to start, play, load out,
drive to hotel, watch TV for an hour,
shower, write, sleep, repeat.

All I can think about lately when I see
an attractive female is how much I wish I
was them, how much I wish their body was
mine.

The last time I had dressed in women's
clothes was 2005. The urge came back and
I could not control it. I wish I had been
born a girl. I always have. I don't know
how to make sense of all this, being married, having a baby in October, being
in this band. How do I reconcile these
feelings?

I can't consciously choose an impossible dream sure to provide only isolation and embarrassment over the life I currently have. But goddamn I would like to.

I daydream of disappearing, dropping off the face of the earth. Take some money out of the bank, get on a plane to some place I won't be found, change my name, grow my hair long, change my appearance, lose weight, shape my body as close as I can to a woman's, cover up my tattoos, start taking hormones, get plastic surgery, my lips, my nose, breasts. Start a new life. Hope for the best. None of it would be easy. Would I be happy? Or would I find myself feeling just as unfulfilled as I do now?

May 16, 2009--Adelaide, Australia

Some nights it doesn't feel good to be touched by strangers; to be standing, eyes closed, singing and have someone drunkenly throw their arm around your neck and start screaming into your face, the repugnant stench of their rancid beer breath filling your nostrils. If I were to say this to anyone, people would think I was an ungrateful asshole, don't bite the hand that feeds. Don't put yourself on a pedestal. Tonight was one of those nights I didn't want to be touched. Sorry.

Chuck Ragan has convinced me to switch
set times with him and close the show each
night. He seems to think this makes sense.
I disagree. He's infinitely more talented
of a solo performer than me. If there's
one thing I hope to learn from this tour
it's how to be gracious.

My alarm is set for 9 AM. I'm going
to wake up, work out, and start the
day. I need to reexamine everything,
rethink every thought, go deep, as deep
as it takes to find the songs I need. I
know they're there. I just need to figure out how to pull them out. I want a
spiritual journey, clean out the trash
from the corners of my brain, drop all
dead psychic weight. I need transforma-
tion, to absorb, transcend, to feel alive.
Forget about the past and move forward
completely. I need to kill Tom Gabel,
destroy his ego.

I'm not gonna do the claps," George Rebelo informed us bluntly
at our first practice with him.

George was a veteran drummer, recording and touring profes-
sionally longer than any of us. His band, Hot Water Music, was
legendary in the punk scene and, being from Gainesville, the
local band we looked up to as the shining example of how to
make a living playing music. Since things with Hot Water Music
had cooled down over the years, George had free time, mostly
picking up bar shifts to get by. The three of us all agreed he was

clearly the best, easiest, quickest, most local option to fill our newly vacant drum seat.

In the middle of our song "Those Anarcho Punks Are Mysterious," there is a bridge where we stop playing and sing over our clapping beat into the next verse. "And we rock, because it's us against them / We found our own reasons to sing / And it's so much less confusing when lines are drawn like that." This was always a part of the set when Warren would shine. He'd stand up on his drum stool, grinning ear to ear, clapping his hands above his head, making sure everyone in the audience joined in. But George let us know right away that he had no intention of doing this. At no point would he be standing up and clapping, he told us.

George was a great drummer, but once again, a drummer with a completely different feel than the last. Instead of being unable to emulate Warren's style, he was often just stubbornly unwilling to. We liked and respected him, but it was immediately obvious that he viewed playing with us as a good career opportunity—there was money in the gig and the chance to work with a legendary producer. He wasn't planning on being an invested member of the band. Why would he? We were being sued, after all.

He would take a smoke break between every three songs during practice. Andrew and I convinced him to attend Crossfit endurance training with us five days a week before practice every morning. We said we wanted to go, and we did, but really, we wanted him to go. Hit a tractor tire with a sledgehammer five times in a row, then drop and do five push-ups, hit the tire 10 times, then 10 push-ups, and so on. Try doing that shit after a long night of binge drinking and weed smoking. I've never thrown up harder.

Our practice studio in Gainesville was a 90-minute drive from my home in Saint Augustine. I started sleeping there during the week, curled up in a sleeping bag on the floor of the gear closet among the amps and guitar cases. When the lights went out, it was a pitch-black tomb. Opening the door every morning to be greeted by the Florida sunshine and humidity was a daily act of violence against myself.

I told Heather I was staying at the studio because I needed the time to work on the album, which was true, but really, it was because I knew it was my last chance to be her. I kept a bag of women's clothes in a locked file cabinet in the studio's loft space. After the band left for the night, I would smoke weed and drink wine and make the space mine, as if the outside world didn't exist. With a baby coming in just a few months, I knew this behavior would have to end before it was born. I'd have to put it behind me forever once I became a father—the wigs, the dresses, the makeup—but if I didn't have this one last chance to be her, I would suffocate.

After a few weeks of rehearsals and demoing with George, it was time for me to head out alone to Los Angeles for preproduction with Butch. The two of us had agreed that I would finish writing the album out there with him, working one-on-one on song structures and vocal melodies before the rest of the band came out. I was looking forward to the time with Butch, and wanted to learn anything and everything he was willing to teach me. Heather agreed to come to Los Angeles when the rest of the band did. We would have the baby there.

I gave myself a full week to make the drive from Florida and loaded up the car with an ounce of weed, two eightballs of cocaine, a cornucopia of assorted pills, and my bag of dresses. No map, just driving west. I had the car windows tinted before leaving, so that I could be her for the whole drive. This was my last hurrah.

I didn't even make it out of Gainesville before I was nose-deep in blow. I stopped at the Gainesville Mall to buy underwear at

Victoria's Secret. I checked into the first hotel across the Georgia state line, desperate to get out of men's clothes. Each day I would check out of my hotel a woman and, before checking into the next one, change outfits in the parking lot, wearing sunglasses to hide the makeup and putting on male attire.

Somewhere around Tucumcari, New Mexico, I got a call from Heather saying she didn't feel well and was going to check herself into the emergency room. I was too fucked up to register what to do. I should have manned up, sobered up, and booked a flight back to Florida. But instead I sat paralyzed in my hotel room until she called back to tell me she and the baby were fine. The doctor said she had just eaten too many avocados.

I rode white lines through a thick cloud of smoke the whole way to California, holding the drugs in my bra. When I hit Barstow, 100 miles outside L.A., I pulled over and threw everything out—$800 worth of clothes I'd bought on the drive west and the empty plastic bags that were once filled with drugs. Goodbye, narcotic breasts. It all went in the dumpster. I prayed that everything else went with it—all of the urges and impulses, all of the shame of a life sneaking around to hide my secret. This was it. I was going to be a man, I told myself; a husband to a wife, a father to a child, a frontman to a band with a hit record. A man.

El Dorado Studio didn't feel as good as Paramount, where we had recorded New Wave three years prior. It felt colder and darker. The ceilings were too high, and we felt small and insignificant under them. The studio intern would light incense and we'd put it out. Then he'd come back and light it again. We'd raise the lights and he'd dim them.

Shortly into the recording process, we also learned that our personalities were not meshing with George's. He came into the studio one day and told us he had some notes on our vocal harmonies. A drummer with notes on harmonies. Fuck me. I realized we had rushed the decision to commit to him, and should have explored more options. Still, when Warren's girlfriend, acting as his lawyer, continued to email us about negotiating the terms of our parting agreement, claiming that her client should no longer be held responsible in the lawsuit, I had no regrets about kicking him out.

George wasn't the only one with suggestions. The label A&R visited the studio one day to hear the new songs and brought with him a long list of terrible ideas, including changes to lyrics, drum beats, and not-so-subtle hints at our physical appearance.

"You know what I fucking hate? Fat people in bands. It's like, lose fucking fifteen pounds before you get your ass up on stage. No one wants to see that shit. Right?"

We got the point. He was telling us to lose weight. Everyone in the studio just sat silently and took it. None of us told him to go fuck himself. I felt like a coward for not kicking him out.

A part of me felt profound disappointment and disillusion while I sat behind the engineer, watching him pitch-correct and paste together my vocal takes. I reconciled it by reminding myself that the words were real, that the emotion behind them was authentic. But we didn't need authentic sounds; this was audio CGI. We needed hits—songs that would get played on the radio and sell to a wide audience. This was what I wanted.

If it wasn't for Butch, I wouldn't have made it through the four-month session. Butch had become a constant in my life. When Heather came out to L.A., we rented an apartment blocks from his house, and he gave me a ride to and from the studio each day. He told me tales from his own band's past. When a song by someone like Nirvana or Smashing Pumpkins came on the radio, he regaled me with stories about recording them. Every tale was filled with trial and tribulation. He encouraged me to consider the lawsuit we were going through as par for the course of choosing a life of rock and roll. Just a rite of passage.

As Heather and I were getting settled into our new Los Angeles apartment, preparing the place for the baby, Butch brought his daughter's old crib over for us to use. He passed it down to us as it had been passed down to him. He even helped me set it up. It was endearing watching this studio genius struggle to figure out how to put it back together, which screw went where. I couldn't help but feel that it was a moment that should have been shared between a father and son, and I wondered how many moments like this I'd missed out on in life. I had a better relationship with my producer than I did with my own father.

8. HIGH PRESSURE LOW

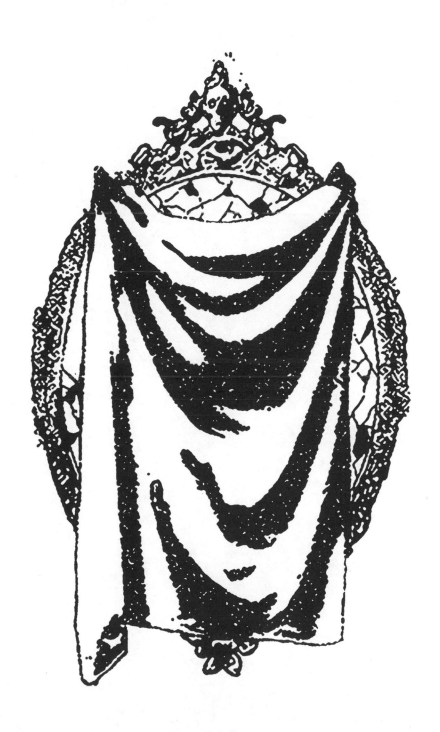

The baby arrived on October 30, Devil's Night, a girl—Evelyn Omneya Gabel. I remember the day well, as she has made me tell her the story many, many times before bed.

"Were you and Mommy at the sushi restaurant?"

Yes, we were eating at the sushi restaurant, right around the corner from our apartment in Silver Lake, when Mommy's water broke. So we went back to our apartment and called our midwife, Mrs. Deborah Frank, and she came over and said, "Yep, the baby is coming, it's time to go to the hospital!"

"And then you drove?"

Yes, so then I put Mommy, with you still inside of her, into the Prius and drove all the way across Los Angeles from Silver Lake to Santa Monica and checked into the hospital. We waited and waited for you to come, but after 27 hours you still wouldn't come out. So the doctors told Mommy she was going to have to have a C-section and they cut you right out. I always knew you were going to be a little girl, but when I saw for sure, I shouted out, "IT'S A GIRL!!!"

The doctors brought you over to this little table under a bright light to keep you warm, and I came over and I said, "Hi, Evelyn, I'm your daddy, and I love you so much." And you reached out just like this and grabbed hold of my pinky finger and I was so happy. Then the doctors handed me scissors and I cut your umbilical cord. They wrapped you up like a little burrito and handed you to me. I walked over to Mommy, holding you, and I said, "Evelyn, this is your mommy." And you smiled a little smile. They finished sewing Mommy back up and brought her into another room. I carried you there and handed you to her and you were so hungry you went straight to latch onto her bey-boo, like this…"Nom, nom, nom, nom."

For three days, our little family stayed there at the hospital. Mommy slept in a bed and you slept in a crib next to her and I slept on a couch. When it was time to leave, I put Mommy and you back into the Prius and drove all the way back across Los Angeles from Santa Monica to Silver Lake, back to our apartment, where you were finally home with us and we were a family.

My little girl Evelyn, always asleep before the end of the story.

———

This sounds like shit."

That was what Tom Whalley, the head of Warner, told me upon first listen of the new album. Told me right to my face. Couldn't have missed hearing it, not with my big ears. "Like shit."

In the days after Evelyn was born, Butch had been busy mixing the album at a little studio in Atwater Village around the corner from our apartments. I'd stop by every day and listen to the progress. Whalley hated what Butch had done with it. He wanted it remixed, and threw $70,000 at us to hire someone else to do so. Fortunately, Butch is a professional and took it in stride. He'd made dozens of major label records, and had learned that this temperamental behavior came with the territory.

Realistically, the odds were very low that we could actually produce a hit. We were right at the end of the era where albums could still sell millions of copies, let alone rock bands, let alone some punk band from Florida. I knew all of this, but what could I do about it? I had to wake up every day and try to make the best of the situation I was in. The label chose the song "I Was a Teenage Anarchist" as the radio single and planned to make a music video for it. The song was our Hail Mary pass; it had to be a hit.

"Do you remember when you were young and you wanted to set the world on fire?"

As much as the album's setbacks and expectations were weighing on me, I couldn't get my mind off of the possibility, no matter how unrealistic, of becoming a woman. It began to consume me. Late at night, after Heather and Evelyn would go to bed, I'd sit on the couch in the living room and watch videos on my computer, testimonials of people who were in various stages of gender transition. I knew how cold and callous this was, but when I saw these people, I judged their appearance and transition results in my head. "That person passes," I'd think. "I don't want to look like that person." "I'd be fine looking like that person." I even researched local psychiatrists that specialized in gender, although I never had the courage to do anything with the information. The idea of opening up to anyone filled me with dread.

Moving to Los Angeles meant that I'd have to travel back to Gainesville, where the rest of the band was, for weeks of practices between tours, with Heather and the baby remaining behind.

I stayed at hotels in the area, and couldn't wait to get done with practice so I could rush back to my room and be her. I became more and more brazen, the longer I stayed. I developed a system. I requested a room on the ground level with a balcony door so that I could walk out to my van in the parking lot. I could leave the door open to not worry about being locked out of my room with a demagnetized hotel key card in full femme. I kept a change of boy clothes in the van, just in case.

At first, I walked only as far as the soda machine down the hall and back. When I pulled the door closed behind me, I heard the lock click shut, and my heart beat out of my chest. Every second spent waiting for the can of soda to drop felt like hours. Emboldened by the success of soda capers, I then walked outside to the van and back in a dress, heels, makeup, and wig. I ventured a bit farther outside my comfort zone each night until I was driving around town, usually ending up at the rehearsal space after hours when I knew no one would be there. I took great care to avoid people. I checked both ways before entering hallways, making sure the coast was clear in either direction before making my move. But when a door opened behind me, I sped up until I could turn a corner and hide. These close calls terrified me.

November 9, 2009--Los Angeles, CA

Another birthday comes and goes.
Twenty-nine years old. Who fucking cares?
Heather made me blow out a candle before
she went to bed. It wasn't on a cake. It
was one of the emergency earthquake can-
dles I'd bought. She just said it was
proper that I should blow out a candle

and make a wish on my birthday. I wished
that in a year from now, I wouldn't feel
the same way as I do now. It's futile, it
really is.

I've realized that even when this lawsuit is over, win or lose, I have been
broken. I have not walked or crawled
through any of this, I have been dragged.
I feel like a failure, a total fucking
failure.

Knowing that there's a bottle of 40
Vicodin in the bathroom drawer is not good
for me. I have no self-control. I just
swallowed my second of the night. I want
to swallow all of them. Good times.

Two-hour-long conference call with the
lawsuit lawyer. Warren has his hand cupped
over the phone receiver and is talking to
people in the background the whole time.
I'm pretty sure he was taking orders at
his restaurant and doing the dishes at one
point. What a fuck. That phone call cost
thousands of dollars.

Is suicide an option? Would my ever-
lasting soul be damned for taking my life
with my own hands, for the sin of running
away from it all? Somehow suicide seems
doesn't seem as cowardly as existing right
now does. It's more like just clearing the
slate. I could be wrong though. Best to
not risk the chance.

December 2, 2009--Flight DL1720

It's unrealistic to think that I can
go on living this way. I'm completely
unhappy. The way I feel inside is never
going to change. This is how I felt when
I was six years old, when I was 14 years
old, and this is how I feel now at 29
years old. Why wouldn't I continue to feel
this way for the rest of my life? A successful career doesn't change it. Marriage
doesn't change it. Having a kid doesn't
change it.

How do I reconcile the person I am now
with the person I want to be? How would
the people in my life handle such a dras-
tic change and how would it change our
relationships? My wife? My mother? My
friends? The producer? The record label?
Our audience? How would making a change
like this affect my daughter's life? So
many unknowns and so many terrifying
possibilities.

How would making this choice change me
psychologically? Would gender liberation
bring me out of depression? Would I no
longer rely on drugs and alcohol as a coping mechanism? Would I still be able to
work as a musician?

What if I made this decision, announced
it to all my friends and family and the
rest of the world, and then I realized it

wasn't really what I wanted and that I was
none the happier for it?

Would I ever be attractive? Pretty, even?

———————

December 29, 2009--Silver Lake, CA

I am incapable of being honest with
myself or anyone else. I hate my life. It
doesn't have to do with Heather. It doesn't
have anything to do with the pressures of
being married and having a kid. It doesn't
have anything to do with currently being
sued for a million dollars. It doesn't have
to do with anything but what's going on
inside of my head. I am suffering from
gender dysphoria.

I didn't enter into my marriage or the
decision to have a child having fully
realized any of this. I thought the dysphoria was behind me. It was only this
past year that I came to the full realization. I think sometimes now about running
away and starting a new life somewhere
alone. I know I could never abandon Evelyn
though and I don't want to lose Heather.

I now fantasize constantly about coming
out and being honest about the way I feel
and really am with everyone I know. I wish
I was brave enough to do that. I know if I
were to choose to transition that I would

```
lose most of the people in my life, if not
all of them. But if this is a decision
I'm serious about making, then now is the
time, while I'm still young and while my
daughter is still young.
     Will I ever pass?
```

Not long after we completed the album at the end of the year, Andrew and Verité announced that they were soon to be joining Heather and me as new parents. The supportive side of me—the side that was a good friend, ecstatic about their news—was gone. Instead, the bandleader side of me—the side that put our careers first—started doing the math. If Verité was three months pregnant, and had six months left to go, that would put her due date in the early summer, right when our new album was scheduled for release. While I feigned excitement and offered them congratulations, in my mind, I saw my battleship sunk. Their pregnancy was an inconvenience. Selfish, even. They hadn't thought ahead like Heather and I had.

The promotional effort and the group solidarity needed to successfully launch an album would be impossible now. We would need to be firing on all cylinders, and it looked like we were down half of them. I would have to find a fill-in bass player, as Andrew would definitely need time off. Not only was this our first album with a new drummer, but we'd now have some faceless bassist up there on stage. Would fans even recognize this band anymore? Would I?

It was waiting for me every morning when I opened my eyes. A tattoo across my wrist: "Ramblin' Boys of Pleasure," the title of a song by my friend Brendan Kelly, which had been lifted from a Pogues song. He and I had gotten matching tattoos of the phrase one night years ago when we were drunk on tour in Dallas with his band, the Lawrence Arms. I don't even remember getting it, just waking up hungover in a hotel bed in Austin next to Brendan, both of us wearing plastic wrap around our new markings. My arms and legs had collected plenty of bad tour tattoos over the years by then. Some I regretted and had covered with thick black bands, but none as much as this one. I saw the word staring back at me every time I looked down, a reminder of the person I never truly felt I was: BOYS.

I woke up one morning and made the decision—I wanted it gone, off my body forever. Whether I realized it or not, this was my first step; the start of my acceptance that I was going to transition into a woman.

9. BAMBOO BONES

Andrew was visibly shaken throughout our whole show in Boston, his fingers trembling as they plucked at his bass. Just minutes before we took the stage, he got the call that Verité was going in for an emergency delivery, at more than two months early.

"What do I do?" he asked me after hanging up the phone. I didn't know what to say.

I could see the panic in his eyes, but like a champ, he powered through the set and then immediately hopped the first plane back to Gainesville.

A fill-in player flew out from Portland in time for the next day's show, a stranger never to be seen again after his duty was fulfilled, but the bus broke down and we had to cancel anyway. I wasn't surprised. Nothing fazed me anymore. Of course the bus broke down, of course the baby came early. This tour was just one more calamity in another disastrous album launch for Against Me!.

I had titled the album *White Crosses* as my homage to Florida and the amphetamines that fueled the writing of it. Lacking the time to put together another cut-and-paste creation of my own, I submitted a "melter" image commissioned from the graphic design artist Steak Mtn. It was a vintage erotica portrait, the subject's face and body dripping away into the scene. The gender identity of the nude model was mangled, blurring into a black and white mélange of flesh and tits. I saw myself in the image, a self-portrait of sorts, a Frankenstein's monster of compartmentalizations.

Unsurprisingly, not only did the label "not get it," they outright hated it. They hammered us for the most arbitrary changes, flower pots in the background taken out or a foreground lamp altered slightly, trying to sway my mind into choosing a new direction. I insisted and tried to take the criticism in stride. I was trying to be receptive to any idea thrown my way on this album by the label, the producer, the engineer, or the manager, but I had a vision, too.

White Crosses was our second major label album to leak before its release date. The label had again scurried to accommodate the blunder, but it was futile. We never found out who leaked it, although everyone, including our own manager, pointed their fingers at me.

"I Was a Teenage Anarchist" was getting radio play, though, which I was told was a big deal. KROQ in L.A. put it in rotation, and it was in the top five in commercial radio in Canada. Good for the song, I thought. I was happy for it, but I didn't feel any ownership over it anymore. It wasn't mine, having been stripped from me by all the compromises I'd made with the team of people working on it. We filmed a video for it on the Venice Beach boardwalk. In one, unbroken slow-mo scene, it depicted several cops beating the shit out of me with nightsticks in front of a crowd of horrified onlookers, as my tribute to the abuse I'd suffered as a teenager at the hands of the Collier County sheriff's office.

"I was a teenage anarchist, but then the scene got too rigid. It was a mob mentality, they set their rifle sights on me. Narrow visions of autonomy, you want me to surrender my identity. I was a teenage anarchist, the revolution was a lie!"

Punks hated the song. They took it as an affront, like I had gotten too famous to be bothered with anarchist politics. We'd play it on tour and there would always be two dickheads in the front row giving us the finger through the entire three and a half minutes.

We had played the song on *The Tonight Show* and left feeling defeated. Due to a camera malfunction, we were asked to play it a second time. I realized the second take wasn't as good, and when the manager made me watch a side-by-side comparison of the two in the monitor, I could tell how disappointed he was. He pushed the producers to use the first take despite whatever they felt had gone wrong, but they refused. Jay Leno introduced us by calling us one of the best punk rock bands ever. He shook our hands afterward and said, "Nice job, gentlemen," and my skin crawled just a little bit. The only consolation was giving a *White Crosses* CD to the show's main guest, Dwayne "The Rock" Johnson, and watching him drive off the Burbank lot in his huge SUV with the windows down, blasting "I Was a Teenage Anarchist" and nodding along.

I had spent the entire release day for the album high as a kite on blow. I woke up in a New York City hotel room and started doing rails off the nightstand first thing in the morning, then went on a verbal attack against a journalist at *Alternative Press*, one of the most historically supportive magazines for us. It ended with me telling him to go fuck himself. It felt purposeful. The magazine was notorious for touching up the musicians on their covers, and I was sick of being forever molded into this frontman

I was not. Yet whenever the offer to be on the cover had been extended over the years, a publicist or manager would pressure me into doing it. I figured if I burned that bridge, and I mean really torched it, I'd never be asked to have my fucking photo taken again.

Then later in the day, while still coked out of my mind, I completely tanked our performance at the rooftop launch party thrown by *Spin*. Our publicist introduced me to Doug Brod after the set, the magazine's editor-in-chief. That's part of the game at events like those; you're there to make fans out of the magazine's staff as much as you are the magazine's readers. I shook Doug's hand and all I could manage to say through my clenched jaw was "I have to go pack up my shit." My publicist was not impressed, and cackled a laugh that indicated to me that the band was dead to him. All of this work had gone into the album, and I was too drunk or high to see it to the end.

And now we were stuck sitting on the side of the highway in a broken-down bus and this tour was going to shit as well. Of course it was.

With Andrew gone for over a month of our dates opening for Silversun Pickups, whose fans didn't like us to begin with, Against Me! became a motley crew of people I barely knew. In addition to our fill-in bass player and our brand new drummer, I'd also brought along other random hires to come aboard to handle keyboards, stage lighting, and various new elements that I hoped would expand our live act and make us more dynamic. I was overcompensating for the loss of what had made us any good in the first place. Some days would go by where the only face I recognized was James's. "I miss Andrew," he told me on the walk back to the bus one night. I agreed, but didn't want to acknowledge it. I was a stranger in my own band.

The only good that came of bringing a crew of strangers

on board was meeting Pope. The first time I saw Pope, he was walking down University Avenue in Gainesville wearing a pair of silver aviator sunglasses. Half of his head was shaved and the other half dyed a mix of blood-red and black. All visible skin was tattooed.

Who's the fucking freak? I thought to myself.

I was on my way to meet up with our crew for the tour we were leaving on the next day. I pulled up in front of the hotel and that freak came walking up to the van. The word "hell" was tattooed on his neck, "dope" and "sick" on his knuckles, and drawings from the comic book *Johnny the Homicidal Maniac* on the tops of his hands with stitching around his wrists. He collected tattoos of the word "cunt" on his leg.

"Hi, I'm Pope, your new lighting designer."

We became fast friends, which is rare for me. He was my buddy. The first tour we did together up in Canada was my favorite tour we'd done since the novelty of touring wore off. Pope was a big part of that.

When the stress of a pending lawsuit and a failing partnership with a record label became overwhelming, Pope was always willing to do stupid shit with me in an effort to keep morale up, like buying pellet guns and turning the front bus lounge into a shooting range, or smoking weed and playing video games until the sun came up. We took ecstasy together in Montreal and got in a street fight with a Canadian junkie. Pope took a punch in the face and laughed wildly. I'll never forget that laugh.

He would throw his hands up in the air and walk away with a scream when he got frustrated.

"Fuck my life!" he would exclaim to himself throughout the day.

The burden was then on me to keep our spirits up. I'd laugh and respond: "Mandatory happiness!"

March 21, 2010--Driving

The Canadian auxiliary guitar player
was 45 minutes late for bus call. A search
team was sent out to look for him and he
was found blind drunk in the alley behind
the bar we had been drinking at earlier.
When we yelled out his name, he jumped
behind a dumpster and tried hiding. He
could barely stand, couldn't walk without
help, and not a word coming out of his
mouth was coherent.

We get him back to the bus and he
pushes past me, grabs two slices of pizza
and goes crawling into his bunk to eat
them. We've asked him several times not
to eat in his bunk. It isn't sanitary. It
makes the sleeping area smell like food.
This was the last straw.

Greg the bus driver suggests we just
kick him to the curb, leave him on the side
of the road. I wanted humiliation. Andrew
grabs the video camera and we all surround
his bunk. We rip the curtain open and there
the slob is, disgustingly drunk chewing on
one pizza slice with the other resting on
his shirtless chest. He tries to get up and
I push him back down, hold him inside the
bunk as we all meow like cats as loudly as
we can until we feel satisfied. His bunk
was then sealed closed with duct tape.

In the morning a small hole has been
burrowed through the duct tape and the

Canadian is nowhere to be found. He makes
himself scarce all day.

We should just send him home but with
only a couple shows left and his return
plane ticket already booked to leave from
the last city on this run, we'll keep him
on with us.

It was a stupid decision to bring a
stranger out on tour to play with us, a
total overcompensation for feeling insecure
with a new drummer and a new album with
songs that have more parts overdubbed onto
them than we can possibly reproduce live as
a four-piece. This is us jumping the shark.

––––––––––

March 26, 2010––Driving

I don't remember what time I went to
bed last night but I do remember drinking
white wine, then red, then whiskey, and
smoking a ton of weed. I keep telling myself I need to chill out and take
better care of myself but I want to hang
out and be social and the social scene on
this tour is fucking high and drunk. This
Canadian run opening for Billy Talent is
how I always imagined our arena touring
would be. Huge audiences, great shows, and
then at night after the crowds leave, the
arena is ours to do whatever we want. We
play cards in smoke-filled locker rooms,

drinking into the early morning hours, talking shit and hanging out, listening to music. I don't want to see it end.

If there's a shopping mall close by on our day off, Pope and I have plans to decorate the back bus lounge. We have a vision. We want the back lounge to be called "Cookie World" and be decorated in an all-cookie theme. Cookie pillows, cookie posters, everything we can find that's cookie-related. The absolute key to Cookie World though will be that there will always be trays of cookies set out for people to munch on. This is what happens when great minds get high.

―――――

May 16, 2010--Saint Augustine, FL

Neither the dress nor the shoes fit. My toes are going numb. I should have tried them on before buying them. If only I was so brave.

The elevator is broken so there's a lot of traffic in the stairwell tonight. I accidentally left my cell phone in the van. I'm going to have to go and get it soon, which I'm nervous about. I'm full-on femme. I'm her. What if the key demagnetizes while I'm out of the room? How would I go to the lobby front desk like this? The simple trip of walking to the van and back will be my first outing. Can I pass? Could I ever?

I'm not happy. Maybe coming out and pursuing this fucked up delusion is the only way to save myself, and instead of spending the rest of my life feeling like I'm a sick pervert or that there's something wrong with me, I could move on and focus on things that are good for me and make me happy. Maybe there's a chance of saving my soul if I follow this path.

I'm sick of lurking around the women's section in department stores feeling like I'm some kind of fucking pervert. I want to be able to buy a dress that fits me.

———————

May 17, 2010--Saint Augustine, FL

I've turned off my cell phone. I need to calm my mind. I need this time to be her. I know that I'll hate myself after a binge like this, I always do.

Is there any difference between this and having an affair? I'm not fucking anyone but myself.

In the time it took me to walk from my hotel room down the stairs to get outside, it started pouring rain. I was going to find a place to sit on the beach and write. Even something as simple as writing in public while her is exhilarating. The sun on my skin feels like an accomplishment.

I think my weight and facial hair are
the biggest obstacles for me in passing.
I wish I were a woman. It's a thought that
no matter how long I go without entertaining it, it always comes back to me.

I don't know how to reconcile those
feelings with my current life, my wife, my
daughter, my family and friends, my band.
I don't think I have the strength to transition. Shaving my legs and painting up
my face is one thing. Hormones and plastic
surgery, changes you can't go back on, are
a different kind of commitment.

I'm in plain sight now, surrounded by
people. Is anyone onto me?

The other guests here at the Holiday
Inn are mostly families and middle aged
tourists. This feels less threatening.
Young adults scare me. They're more likely
to notice and less likely to be polite
about it if they do.

These tits aren't real. This is just a
wig.

I'm just a faggot in a dress with my
dick tucked between my legs.

———————

July 20, 2010--Houston, TX

What would be my biggest obstacle in
transitioning? Coming out to my family,
my friends, the people I work with, the

public at large? The physical changes of
hormones, electrolysis, and plastic surgery? Passing? I don't want to embarrass
myself. I don't want to go through the
pain of coming out to only end up a bald
woman. Do I have the hair for it? I don't
care about passing by anyone else's standards but my own. I want to look in the
mirror and believe that I'm looking at a
woman. I want to feel like a woman. That
is my biggest fear. That I would never
truly feel like a woman. I don't want to
be a joke. I don't want to ruin my life. I
don't want to be ashamed. I want to draw a
line in between the past and the present.
I want a new life. I want to be happy. I
want revenge. I want to take back control.
What's the alternative? I don't want to
settle for a half-life.

In a strange way, my dysphoria started to become a sense of
empowerment through all of my career failures. What had in
the past always felt like a vulnerability had now become the one
thing keeping me going, an ace up my sleeve of sorts. It was a
secret that was mine alone, something that no lawyer or manager
or label head could touch because it existed only in my mind. It
was one thing about myself I knew to still be true.

There was one other thing I could make sure no one could
take. When it started to become clear that *White Crosses* was not
going to save us financially, I had the foresight to buy a house in
Saint Augustine. I'd done research and learned that Florida law
shelters property from lawsuits. Even if I was taken to my last
dime by legal fees, my house would still belong to me. Heather,

Evelyn, and I would always have a home that was ours, no matter what happened to the band. I was excited to start packing up and leave Los Angeles behind, though Heather hated Florida. She tried to put on a happy face, but I knew how miserable she was about the idea of returning.

Andrew jumped back onto the tour after a few weeks and, although I was still annoyed with his timing, I recognized that new parent glow about him and was empathetic as a recent father myself. I missed my daughter terribly on tour. I would watch videos I had of her on my phone repeatedly throughout the day. I studied the way she moved her hands and the way her eyes paid attention. I loved the way her tiny little neck supported her pumpkin head, and most of all I loved her beautiful smile. I thought of me, her, and Heather, a family. I thought of us in our new house. I thought of Saint Augustine, the white sand shores, the tips and towers of Flagler College, the Spanish Fort, the tourists on King Street, and the merry-go-round that we would one day soon ride together. It was a feeling of safety. There were still a lot of shows left to play, a lot of miles yet to cover, but I was coming home to all that soon.

Though *White Crosses* charted higher on the Billboard list in its first week, overall album sales were on the decline. While this normally would have been another tremendous disappointment for the label, they had bigger problems to deal with. Right after the album's release, Tom Whalley was ousted as head of Warner, replaced by Lyor Cohen, who had previously led Def Jam Recordings. Cohen came in and gutted the place. Our publicist, our product manager, and almost everyone else on our team were given silver parachutes and left. Our A&R contact got promoted to the head of Sire, and I knew we wouldn't be much of a priority anymore. We were about to slip through the cracks. The promotional campaign was finished, dead in the water before we had the chance to even do a headlining tour in support of the album. I got the call from the manager letting me know all of this a day before we were supposed to fly to Australia for a tour, followed directly by one in the UK with the Toronto band Fucked Up. I hung up the phone and called a band meeting in my room at the Garland Hotel in Los Angeles.

James, Andrew, and George came over and sat down on the beds. I offered them the only solution I thought made sense at the moment, the last option I saw left.

"It's over," I told them. "We're done."

I had been humbled by it all, beaten down by the lawsuit and too tired to keep fighting.

My plan had failed. I thought that if I fully devoted myself to making an album—if I gave every ounce of my soul to it without reservation; if I worked cooperatively with all the people involved in the project; if I listened without cynicism to advice; if I invested financially in the band and its infrastructure, the stage show, the crew; if I was accommodating to press and radio, willing to try to put a positive spin on the answer to every question asked; if I opened myself up and tried to have a good time while onstage and connect with the crowd—I thought that maybe if I did all of these things, it would pay off and the album would be successful and we would stand a chance of fighting this lawsuit. But I thought wrong. I felt defeat, and it burned.

I told the guys I'd be going back home the next morning and would start selling off my equipment to make payments, and recommended they do the same. No one really argued. What was there to argue? The writing was on the wall for Against Me!. George was quick to distance himself from the band. "Well, you all have got some things to figure out." The emphasis was on *you*. He was already on a lifeboat, rowing away from our sinking ship.

They bought plane tickets back to Florida, but I opted to rent a car at the airport. It meant something symbolically that I drive back on my own. A year ago, I had packed up and driven west alone to begin my quest of making the album that was meant to save us, but I'd failed. It seemed only right that I do my penance by returning the way I came.

Fifty-six hours and 2,400 miles from Los Angeles to Saint Augustine, the rental car's stereo broken. Minimal stops for gas and bathroom breaks. As I pushed the speed limit, the road beside me blurred into a flickering stream of fading memories. The highways that once served as paths to endless possibilities now were a gloomy procession for the loss of a feeling. I clenched the wheel and pressed my foot further on the gas pedal. I met my blue eyes in the rearview mirror. "We're never going home," I scoffed aloud at the naiveté of my former self, but there was no one there to hear it.

The band was worth nothing now. Less than nothing, in fact. All the years I'd spent building it up felt like a lie. I leaned on the pedal even harder. Fifty-six hours and 2,400 miles to think about everything I'd lost, and how I could ever get it back, or kill the son of a bitch who stole it from me. I crossed over the Saint Johns County line through a thick morning fog.

I was inhaling the burning scrapings of resin out of a bong while listening in on a conference call with the managers and lawyers when they told me the lawsuit was over. They assured me that it was done for good, but I didn't trust it. It was late October, and this lawsuit had consumed me for over two years. It was hard to believe it could actually come to an end. Even if it was finally finished, the damage had been done. Against Me! had been declared dead.

Though we were able to cancel our Australia and U.K. dates, management was insistent that we honor obligations we'd made to play three radio festivals to end the year, threatening that reneging would "irreparably damage our careers" should we ever decide to play music again, and could even result in another lawsuit. The problem was, George had already committed to a tour with Hot Water Music. So we'd need someone to fill in for three shows.

I remembered reading that the New York hardcore band Madball had recently parted ways with their drummer, Jay Weinberg. The story made news because the split was not on amicable terms, leading to some drama. We had met Jay through the Bouncing Souls. He was a fan who had been coming to our shows for years. He even used to jump in and take over drums for Warren on the last song in our set when he'd see us play. To us, he was just a young kid from New Jersey, only 20 years old, but he had an impressive resume. His father, Max, was the longtime drummer for Bruce Springsteen and the E Street Band. When Jay was a teenager, he got to keep his father's seat warm for a few dates due to a scheduling conflict that kept Max busy as bandleader for *The Tonight Show* when Conan O'Brien took over the hosting gig from Leno. Guitarist Steve Van Zandt once attributed Jay's skills behind the kit to the Weinberg DNA. If he had the chops to jam with Springsteen, certainly he could pull off an Against Me! song.

Jay knocked his audition with us out of the park. I asked him to learn 15 songs, but he showed up knowing the whole catalog; songs even Andrew, James, and I had forgotten how to play. He had a style that was frenetic and wild, like he was putting his whole body into his playing. Best of all, he was not above doing the claps. He was in. We sent word to management that we'd worked out a solution for the shows. They offered congratulations in response, and in the same breath told us they were dropping us from their roster as clients.

Against Me! felt both born anew and like the same old prison sentence. We were ending the year with no lawsuit, but also no manager, no label, and a big pile of debt. We had a new drummer, but even that came with caveats. Jay's comparative youth both motivated us and was a total pain in the ass. After our first practice, Andrew, sweaty and winded, said, "I'm gonna have to start hitting the gym again to keep up." But we also quickly realized we were dealing with a spoiled brat. That was OK, we thought; we'll take him under our wing, we'll show him how to be cool, like our kid brother, something his privileged upbringing and Daddy's deep pockets could never buy him.

Now did not seem like a time we could start over from the beginning. Now did not seem like the time to rise to the occasion, if ever there was one. But the three radio shows with Jay went better than we expected. Neither James, Andrew, nor I wanted to quit. Our booking agent brought us an offer to do a headlining tour, one to finally support *White Crosses*, which the label had generously given us the rights to in full so we could rerelease it on our own label.

Our schedule was still comparatively light to what it had been in the past, and I wanted to keep it that way. I told our booking agent to keep us busy enough to get the band back on its feet financially, but nothing too heavy.

Personally, I recognized that I needed to make a decision: to commit to gender transition, or not. I wanted time to reflect at home, to be around my wife and daughter, to sit on my back porch, drink beer, smoke weed, and think. If I still felt the same way at year's end, I was going to accept myself and go ahead with the transition.

10. PARALYTIC STATES OF DEPENDENCY

I was brushing my teeth in the mirror one morning when I noticed the deep wrinkles on my forehead and the dark circles under my eyes. Time had dug itself in over the years. I was bloated, my complexion was bad, and I looked permanently tired. At 30 years old, I had put almost half my life into this band. All the hard living was catching up to me. The nights spent sleeping on dirty floors, the drugs, the week-long benders—all of it was staring right back at me. I wore the face I'd earned.

I opened the cabinet, took out a bottle of Rogaine, and massaged a glob into my scalp with my fingertips. The bright lights of the bathroom exposed patches of white scalp under greasy strands of thinning brown hair. I didn't know if the hair loss was from testosterone or high stress levels of cortisol. The longer I put off the idea of transitioning, the less realistic the possibility seemed.

That year, 2011, would become the year that I eased myself into the idea of transitioning. The steps would be small and subtle at first, with things like growing out my hair, losing a few pounds, and continuing to laser off the tattoo on my wrist. Each of these little steps was an effort to be happier with the person I saw in the mirror.

January 12, 2011--3:12 AM

I'm adrift out here, lost at sea. There's no hope, no difference, no point. I'm trying to appreciate that hour and a half on stage and it's been great, don't get me wrong, but an hour and a half of living out of 24 in a day doesn't seem excusable. How quickly we lose faith in ourselves.

No towels to dry my hands or face after washing. A filthy backstage dressing room in a filthy club. I haven't showered in how many days now?

I'm not feeling the same desperate urge to be feminine as I did a week ago. I just want to feel clean. It doesn't feel like it could ever be a reality, so really, what's the point? Jason Thrasher sent a first cut of the video he directed for "Because of the Shame." There are shots towards the end, live shots when I'm drenched in sweat, where my hair loss is noticeable. I've been using Rogaine but realistically what are the best results I can hope for? I can shave my legs and put on a dress, have doctors fill my chest with silicone, I can pay for them to chop my cock off and build

me a plastic cunt, but if I'm bald, what's
the point? I don't want to wait until all
of my youth is gone. I don't want to end
up a sad, old tranny.

I feel so much love for my wife. I know
how lucky I am to have someone as understanding as she is but would she understand this? Lately all I can think about
is how much I want to fuck her. I wish
that could be enough for me always.

———

January 21, 2011--Driving to Huntsville,
AL--12:19 PM

Pope was up on a ladder at the Exit/
In venue in Nashville, removing gels and
focusing lights. A venue stagehand was
holding the ladder below and let go for a
second, the ladder slipped off the rafter
lip it was resting against and Pope fell
20 feet to the venue floor, breaking and
dislocating the majority of bones in his
right foot and ankle.

I was backstage when it happened. I
heard the crash and the screaming that
followed. Pope was taken by ambulance to
the emergency room. He was back before set
time, hobbling into the room on crutches,
leg in a cast, fucked up, and in tremendous pain but still keeping a sense of
humor about it. That's just Pope. I joked

with him to stop trying to steal the sympathy spotlight away from me and my aching back.

"Fuck my life," says Pope.

He wants to stay out on the road, he doesn't have anywhere else to go, no one else to take care of him. I'm not sure this is the best idea. It'd be different if we were in a bus but being in the van is too difficult for him. The band's insurance is going to cover surgeries and rehabilitation. There's a place outside Dallas we can get him to in a couple days.

January 28, 2011--Phoenix, AZ

While sound-checking today, Jay looked over his drumkit and asked me to move a few feet to the side. It took me a few seconds to realize why--he wanted to be center-stage. After a show the other day, the venue's lighting guy came up to me and made a comment that struck me as odd.

"Different lighting setup than the last time you guys were here, huh?"

"I'm sorry?" I asked, confused.

"All the lights on the drummer, that's new."

Now that I thought of it, the stage had been much darker than usual. I approached Jay about it later on the bus.

"Did you tell the lighting guy to point all the house lights at you tonight?" I asked.

"Yeah," he replied in a tone that made the question seem so obvious that it was like I'd asked him if he was the drummer.

———————

February 27, 2011--Chicago, IL

Last night at the bar I outed myself to Brendan. I woke up this morning with disconnected memories of the conversation. "Did I really say what I think I said last night?" I messaged him in the morning to confirm. I really did. It was the end of the night and we were both wasted gone. I told him everything.

"I'm a transsexual. I've always been a transsexual. I want to transition genders and I don't know how to tell Heather. I'm terrified of what this would do to my family and life."

Brendan had been the first person to read into my lyrics deeply enough to pick up on what they meant and call me on it, very publicly on TV. In between Lawrence Arms tours, he landed a gig hosting a show on a local TV network in Chicago, *JBTV*, and we were his guests back in September. He had done his research and wasted no time getting into it.

"So, Tom...do you put on panties when you're at home?" he asked. My face turned hot and red and I started to laugh nervously.

"Ha ha, what?"

"Well, it's been a pervasive theme throughout your records. You've sung about dressing up in women's clothes, the idea of gender non-conformity."

"Yeah, gender confusion is a topic that fascinates me, for sure," I said, hoping we could move on to a new topic which it seemed like we were doing as he turned to James.

"James, can I ask you a question?" Brendan said. Oh thank God. "Did Tom just avoid my question about dressing up in panties?" Fuck! My nervous laughter contin- ued and I blurted out some joke about pre- ferring boxer-briefs.

So last night, I told him. Now he knows everything. Brendan promises me the secret's safe with him and I naively think I believe him. I'm panicked now but it was such a relief to speak those drunken words last night, to emotionally unload on some- one, anyone, relief.

———

March 4, 2011--Minneapolis, MN

"It's necessary to lose all hope."-- Jean-Paul Sartre, *The War Diaries*

I'm working my way through *The War Diaries of Jean-Paul Sartre*. It's comforting to hear someone obsess the same way that I do. He makes and breaks promises to himself about not drinking alcohol and following certain diets the same way I do. He obsesses over self-imposed writing routines. He picks apart the people around him.

Sartre's commitment to journal-keeping has reinvigorated my own. I had previously questioned the purpose behind continuing to keep a journal. I'm not sure it has improved my writing ability and if not what's the point?

It is not unrealistic to think that within five years' time I could be a woman. I will be 35 years old, still much youth left to live.

The thought of the surgeries terrifies me. It's going to hurt a lot more than I think.

Standing onstage last night I could feel the fullness of my inhibition. I have no idea who I am up there. How am I supposed to connect to an audience in such a state? Something needs to break. I can't keep diffusing with coping mechanisms.

Will all of these thoughts ever not seem totally fucking ridiculous?

There is a change happening in me, the results of which have not even begun to manifest. I want to believe in destiny and

I want this to be mine. For what other
reason would I be born this way? What an
embarrassing truth to know about myself.
I've never dealt with embarrassment well.
I've always been sort of a coward.

The drummer insisted that the tour manager call his father. He was demanding
Jordan call 911 last night once we had
gotten to the hotel because he had twisted
his ankle at the show. Jordan refused,
saying that it was fucking ridiculous to
expect an ambulance to come out for a hurt
foot, one that the drummer had been fine
to walk on all night until then, and that
we'd go to a clinic in the morning. The
drummer's father tells Jordan that his son
"is a star and needs to be treated that
way."

"Do your job!" Jordan is scolded.

When we picked the drummer up from an
orthopedic center, he came walking out
in a comically large, full leg brace. The
prognosis? A sprained ankle, like we all
guessed. He doesn't hold much favor with
the group right now. Everyone unanimously
agrees that a) He's a pussy and b) He's a
self-entitled spoiled brat.

He tries taking the leg brace off a
couple hours later because it's uncomfortable and I yell at him that after all his
bullshit he better fucking keep wearing it.

The drummer thinks we give a shit who
his dad is and who his dad knows. We don't.

Andrew, James, and I compared notes on
how much of a brat we think Jay is over
dinner at Pizza Luce. We all agree we can
make it to the end of the year with him
but as for making a record as the four
of us, there's no way it's ever going to
happen.

My wife tells me that her father is
pressing for us to visit New Orleans in
April. Pope is also possibly getting out
of the rehabilitation center he's in and
is saying he might take us up on the
offer to come stay in Florida for a couple
weeks.

————

March 10, 2011--Gainesville, FL

Stopped by a group of drunk fans in the
lobby while waiting for the elevator.

"What are you doing staying in this
dump?!?!?!?" They ask for a picture. Jordan
abandons me and continues to his room.

"Cut your hair and move back to Florida!" they tell me after I pose with them
for photos.

This hotel room is a prison cell. What
am I doing here besides falling apart?
Talking to myself in the bathroom vanity
mirror. Watching TV and nursing a beer. I
can't help but wonder how different of a
person I would have turned out to be had

I simply been born her. I would be happy
and not manic at all. What if I had come
to these conclusions years ago, when I was
younger, less attached?

There are moments when I believe it
and I can visualize myself as her, fully
female, rare moments when life does not
seem so daunting. I can imagine an emotional wall coming down and a part of me
finally coming to life.

———————

April 14, 2011--Saint Augustine, FL

Pope was only 26 years old and now he's
dead and there's nothing any of us can do
about it. All he did was break his fucking foot, he wasn't supposed to die when
we left him in Dallas. He was supposed to
have surgery, get a cast, and be back out
on the road with us by summer.

It was the insurance-provided assisted
living doctors that killed him. They
told him he was schizophrenic. Started
feeding him psychiatric drugs. They
over-medicated him. Too many pills. His
body couldn't take it. He wasn't crazy. He
just wasn't meant for Texas.

They won't release any of his records to
us, only to family. Pope didn't have much
family left, just his older brother and
grandmother. He told us all his parents

were dead. It wasn't until after Pope died
we found out his father was still alive.
None of them are going to chase this.

I feel responsible. We left him. It wasn't
supposed to be a big deal. It was just a
broken foot, a busted ankle. Heather had
been talking to him while he was in the
hospital. We told him to come stay with us.

He was incoherent whenever I'd hear from
him. It was like you could tell the drugs
were kicking in. I was too self-obsessed to
care, too focused on my failing career. Too
busy being full of shit and uninspired. So
fucking original. So fucking wasted. It's a
rare thing to meet someone out on the road
that you connect with. It's such a rare and
beautiful thing to find a true friend out
there on the road. I failed him.

Pope, I'm sorry, so very sorry.

———————

April 18, 2011--Saint Augustine, FL

Rough, nightmare-filled sleep last
night. Evelyn and I took our usual walk
in the morning before breakfast. I can't
focus. I need to start working on something, anything to be productive. That's
how I grieve, I need distraction while my
subconscious works my feelings out.

Heather and I have been fighting. I
don't understand how she's taking Pope's

death harder than me. She never toured
with Pope. I know they talked on the phone
in the weeks prior to his death but other
than that they had been physically in each
other's presence maybe five or six times
and only for a couple hours. She's taken
to calling him "Popey," a nickname none
of us ever knew him by. It almost feels
exploitative or payback for the way I processed C.C.'s death.

Pope's funeral is Friday in Oklahoma City. I've suggested to Heather that
we find a friend we can bring along to
watch Evelyn while we're at the services.
I think Evelyn is too young to go to
the funeral, both for her sake and ours.
Heather disagrees.

I'm trying to stay as sober as possible. I know I'll just get more angry if I'm
drunk. We're out of weed. There's no buffer
between us, everything seems amplified, too
loud. I'm emotionally spent. I can't remember
the last time I felt truly inspired, when
the words came to me faster than my pen
could write them, the feeling I live for.

Goddamn, I miss my dead friend.

April 23, 2011--Oklahoma City, OK

It's fitting that we've had to come and
go to Oklahoma City by way of connection

in Dallas. Pope had to do the same. Texas
is the reason...that Pope's dead.

Visitation with Pope was from 8 to 12
before the 2 PM service. Heather and I
went with Evelyn down to the Eisenhour
Funeral Home in Blanchard, OK but not
before fighting for a half-hour in the
hotel parking lot. I didn't want to take
Evelyn. I didn't want her to see his body.
I didn't want her to see me break down.

I was silent the whole drive there. I
was angry and I wasn't prepared mentally
to see Pope. Holding onto Evelyn as we
walked through the funeral home doors I
was already crying. As I walked up to Pope
laying in his flat black casket Evelyn
started screaming "NO, NO, NO, NO, NO, NO!"
Heather took her outside.

Pope was dressed in his black pea
coat, the coat he was wearing when I met
him. He was wearing a priest collar. His
nails were painted black, his face white
with powder, still wearing his lip ring.
The only thing out of the ordinary about
him was that his hair had been washed. I
touched his hand and it was cold and hard
like marble.

I kept staring at his chest, thinking that I could see it rising and falling
with breath. I kept staring at his face,
waiting for the life to return to it, waiting for his lips to part into a smile.
Waiting for the joke to end.

Heather and I took turns with Pope while the other stayed outside with Evelyn. I don't know why but the thought occurred to me that Heather may have kissed Pope, there alone in the viewing room. Considering how emotional she was I could see her needing some kind of closure or significance to the moment.

When visitation hours ended, before the funeral service started, we came back to the hotel to meet up with the rest of the band. Heather put Evelyn down for a nap while the Jameson bottle and Valium pills started getting passed around. I had James pick me up a pack of Camel Lights when he stopped for the whiskey.

At the funeral home, friends were seated first on the left side of the room, with the right reserved for family. There were more friends than family in attendance and once the left side was full, the ushers began filling up the right.

Pope's friend Jeremy officiated the funeral service. He told the story of how he met Pope. His band Shiny Toy Guns was going on tour and they needed an LD. He had gotten a hold of Pope's old boss Robin saying that he needed someone who was both "completely out of their mind" and "willing to work for nothing." Robin said he knew just the guy.

Jeremy talked about the first impression Pope made upon meeting him, the feeling of

immediate connection, which I too felt the
first time I met Pope. The tattoos, the
voice, the personality, Pope was one of a
kind.

He joked about Pope's smell, a mix of
body odor and Old Spice and how he could
never keep his shoes tied, his pants
always either falling down or full of
holes. One time Pope left on a tour of
Europe with Shiny Toy Guns with nothing but a Blockbuster Video card in his
wallet.

Pope's brother spoke too. I felt bad for
him beyond the obvious reasons of loss.
Pope never spoke kindly of his brother,
their relationship was strained. I'm sure
all of Pope's friends were given the same
impression. Pope's brother must have been
able to sense that from the room. Regardless of anything though they were brothers
and doesn't that mean something? Shouldn't
death forgive?

I thought of my own brother, whom I am
also distant from and the way I would feel
in attendance at his funeral surrounded by
his current friends. I wouldn't know any
of them but they would probably all have
an impression of me, an opinion based on
whatever my brother had told them. What
would that be?

There was a photo montage shown, pictures of Pope throughout his life projected onto a screen. Pope as an infant.

Pope as a child. Pope as a teenager. Pope as a husband. Pope as a friend. Pope at work as a lighting director. He had a true gift as an LD, a total savant, a da Vinci. I had seen some of the pictures before, I was in a couple of them too.

For the finale to the service, the lights were turned off in the room. Fog machines shot off and filled the room with haze as a light show was projected onto Pope's open casket and Marilyn Manson's "The Beautiful People" was blasted at stun volume. It was perfect. Pope would have loved it.

When the song ended, everyone lined up to say a final goodbye to Pope's face. Heather was crying uncontrollably. Her lack of composure kept mine intact. In the parking lot outside of the funeral home everyone drank and smoked. I went in to give Jay a hug and I could tell by the look on his face that he didn't want me to hug him while smoking a cigarette. He didn't want me to get ash on his expensive tailored suit. It was a telling sign of character that I'll never forget or forgive.

I had never been part of a funeral procession before. I can only imagine how funny Pope would have thought it was that two Oklahoma Highway Patrol Officers were giving him an escort through the city, letting him blow through every red light.

Pope's family had arranged for a preacher to give a graveside sermon. Pope would have hated it. The preacher didn't know Pope and his speculation about the type of person Pope was came off as insulting.

We all watched Pope's coffin as it was lowered into the ground. Flowers, cigarettes, and joints were all thrown on top of it before a backhoe and four gravediggers covered him up forever.

It was then that I understood the finality of death, as all of Pope's friends walked their separate directions away from the freshly buried grave. I wondered if Pope was crying out for everyone not to leave, please stay, please stay. Please, stay.

I thought about the absolute darkness surrounding Pope, the complete and total darkness that I am not yet ready to know.

April 26, 2011--Gainesville, FL

It's a manic episode. I'm prisoner until the ride's over. I offer little to no resistance.

Shopping for women's clothes is emotionally exhausting. How many stores did I go to today?

I'm looking for the most ideal shopping situation, an empty store with no one watching. There's always a certain amount of embarrassment involved in the transaction. I can always feel the cashier's judgment.

I'm never able to fully think through what I'm about to buy. I'm too worried someone I know will see me. Trying on clothes is not an option. So I end up hating everything I buy or it just doesn't fit. I've been thinking about getting a P.O. Box for shipping. I would need a debit card or credit card not linked to my joint bank account with my wife so I wouldn't have to explain the charges on our bank statement to her.

I don't like hiding things.

I don't like feeling like I'm having an affair.

I hope someday to be able to share this side of me with Heather and have her accept it, but I'm not ready yet.

I've never stayed at this motel before. It is a true shithole but it's cheap.

I bought women's clothes at Sears today. How embarrassing is it to be a closeted transsexual buying women's clothes at Sears?

It's safe though, no one will see me there. Who the fuck shops at Sears?

The cashier, a frumpy middle aged woman, was breathing through her mouth with her nose closed while she rang me up so she wouldn't catch my sick.

She seemed afraid of the clothes, only
touching them with the very tips of her
fingers.

No questions asked though, there are
usually questions.

The whole exchange is silent.

Not a word spoken between us.

The whole time I think about Pope, and
how he never cared what anyone thought of
him. I think about how short life is and
how there's nothing wrong with being a
freak. Rough surf on the coast today, wish
I could have spent the whole day alone
with you.

Will I ever pass? I don't really care
anymore.

In the summer of 2011, Against Me! got booked on a tour
opening for Blink-182 and Rancid. Even though I was in my 30s,
being around Tim Armstrong and Lars Frederiksen made me
feel like a punk teenager all over again. Every time I saw their
faces, I thought back to that night I first saw them on MTV in
Naples—a place I never thought I'd get out of—and how surreal
it was that I was now sharing a stage with them.

August 26, 2011--4:22 PM

Blink-182 all have separate dressing
rooms. There are signs backstage instruct-
ing crew and security under no circumstances to stop them, talk to them, or
look at them in general. Rancid's dressing

room is right next door to ours, and they
have a much more open vibe. I've become
fast friends with Lars, despite my being
intimidated, as he was one of my idols
when I was young. Rancid was my favorite
band when I was 14. Lars is approachable
and easy to talk to. He also seems to
speak with irony and sarcasm, the language
I know best.

I saw him sitting on the couch in his
room and called him over to come play some
Swingin' Utters songs on guitars with me.
Lars produced their debut album, *Streets
Of San Francisco*, a favorite of mine. Lars
couldn't remember any of the songs, so
we started playing Rancid songs instead.
I was on bass, Lars on guitar. We played
"Hyena" together, a song my first punk
band covered hundreds if not thousands
of times. Tim walked into the room and I
started shaking, I was so nervous. I lost
the strength in my fingers to even hold
down the strings. Still, Tim said he was
impressed.

"It's all in the wrist."

I'm still too in awe of Tim Armstrong
to say anything directly to him. It's so
incredible to be on tour with them.

Some jerk threw a drink on me while
I was watching Blink-182 play from the
audience. He approached me as a fan of my
band. We shook hands and then he started

leaning in too close, spitting in my face
about how much he hated Blink-182, and how
he couldn't believe we were on this tour.
He only came for Rancid and us.

I told him politely that I respected his
opinion, but I liked Blink-182 and just
wanted to watch the show. He looked at me,
offended, and then dumped his drink on
my head. I chased after him, pissed off,
tried to get security to do something.
Andrew and James got in the middle of
us before a fight could happen. Security
escorted him out of the arena as he was
threatening to stab me.

I know that if it would have been me
who threw the drink and started shoving people, I would have been arrested
for assault and possibly sued. Frustrating
that incidents like this make me regret
going out into the audience to watch the
show. It's less hassle to just hang out
backstage and not see anything.

We signed our paperwork, effectively ending our deal with Sire
Records and bringing an official close to the end of our five-year
major label experiment that came within an inch of killing us.
There was an offer on the table from Epitaph Records for our
next album, and another offer to sign a distribution deal with
RED, giving us the ability to start our own label. My pride was
steering me away from Epitaph. It was a reliable independent

punk label, famous for releasing albums by bands like Rancid and NOFX, but I worried that it was where the major label rejects went to die.

It was a risk, but we signed the distribution deal, giving us the capability and capital to start a record label, which I called Total Treble. If we failed, at least it would be on us. But if we succeeded, then we'd be successful on our own terms. And most important to me, I would own the masters of whatever we produced. Not only did I want to release this next album, I wanted to record it, too. For two albums I'd learned what it was like to make concessions to labels, managers, and lawyers. Now was my chance to make up for it. I wanted full control.

I was also paying homage to Butch. After everything he taught me, I wanted the chance to apply his recording theories and test my own. The records we made together were the closest I'd get to going to college. Now I'd graduated, and I was on my own.

I had already started writing some songs for a new album and had been slowly sharing bits of them with the band. They were all centered around the idea of transitioning. It wasn't what I set out to write, but gender was all I could think about, the dream of transitioning.

With the money from the RED deal, I rented an old abandoned post office I planned on converting into a studio on State Road 207 in Elkton, Florida, which is nowhere, just a curve in the road on my drive between Saint Augustine and Gainesville. I had struggled to find a suitable spot, a standalone brick building where I could be as loud as I wanted. The second I saw the post office, I knew it had the magic. I signed a rental lease for $500 a month right on the spot.

"What is it you do again?" asked the suspicious woman renting the building.

"I'm an artist."

The studio needed work. The mildew-ridden blue industrial carpet was a stained mess, and would have to be torn up and replaced with laminate wood flooring. Ceiling tiles and insulation would have to be replaced; walls would need to be built to create a separate control room and live room. Once I realized the place would require more renovations than I could handle myself, I did something a bit underhanded. I called both my brother and my father to ask if they would come down and help me with the work. The two hadn't spoken in half a decade, following their falling-out. Neither of them knew the other would be coming to the studio.

It was awkward at first, but it's amazing how fast beer can mend things among the Gabel boys.

"Here, Mark, you want a beer?" my dad asked, offering over a can of Miller Lite.

"No, I'm good," my brother responded coldly, turning his six-foot-six frame away from our father, focusing on organizing his toolbox.

I could sense how fast this whole setup was going south, so I quickly broke the tense silence. "I'll have a beer, Dad! Hell, I'll have two!"

Once I was halfway through chugging down a cold one, my brother softened and accepted a beer, too. My dad just wanted to share a beer with his two sons, and I wanted to give that to him. All I wanted was to share a beer with my dad and brother.

It felt good to kill two birds with one stone—getting my studio in shape and mending things between my father and brother. But there was a hidden agenda behind it for me. As I felt my desire to transition grow stronger, I was starting to see it as inevitable. I didn't know how either of them would take it, or what it would do to my respective relationships with them. As we hammered away at drywall, collecting sawdust and paint on our Carhartts and finishing off a case of beer, I knew in my heart that this would be the last time the three of us would ever be together as men, the way fathers and sons are.

It was just before midnight on the last day of 2011. We were between songs onstage in Atlanta, Georgia. There was that familiar December 31 air of anticipation in the room, with the crowd eagerly waiting to christen a fresh year. I was as eager as they were. It felt like an official ending to a chapter for me.

I checked the time. 11:59 PM. "Fuck it," I mouthed to myself, and charged the microphone stand.

"Will you guys indulge me for a second?" I asked the room to a smattering of drunken applause. "I just want to end the year in a really fucking selfish way." I ran my fingers through my sweaty hair, which had grown down past my ears over the last few months. "If you've got to start counting, go ahead and start counting," I told them. "I'm just gonna play a new song real quick."

The faces before me looked confused as to what I was about to do. Not even the rest of the band knew what I was doing. It didn't matter. This wasn't for anyone else but me. I started to strum the opening chords to what would become the final track on the album I was writing, which I planned on titling *Transgender Dysphoria Blues*. "This song is called 'Black Me Out,'" I told them.

It was just me and my guitar, exorcising the demons of years past. As I finished the first verse, the room erupted. People cheered and whistled, confetti trickled down, Andrew and James popped bottles of champagne behind me and passed them around the front row. I smiled and kept playing, shouting the words to compete with the volume of the celebration, and pretending the energy was for me.

"I don't want to see the world that way anymore, I don't want to feel that weak and insecure. As if you were my fucking pimp, as if I was your fucking whore. Black me out."

For another two minutes, I clenched my eyes shut and powered through this song no one had ever heard, and to which no one could sing along. Couples continued to kiss, as though I was serenading them with a three-chorded "Auld Lang Syne." For them, it was background music for their toasts to another year gone by. I was toasting, too. It was a farewell song. This was the night I said goodbye to Thomas James Gabel.

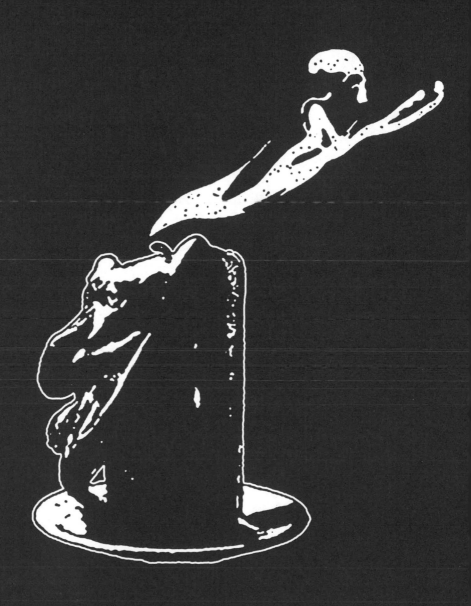

Our house in Saint Augustine sat where the Tolomato River meets the Atlantic Ocean. The kitchen looked out onto sprawling acres of marsh. The Florida air was always humid with salt. In the distance was the Fountain of Youth, the site where Ponce de León was said to have landed in 1513. The fountain was really just a spring coming up from the aquifer beneath the soil. What the Spanish explorer once thought to be the key to eternal life was now the water that locals drank, showered, pissed, and shit in. I'd spent the last couple of years looking out the windows of Butch's hillside home in Silver Lake, onto a Los Angeles I could not conquer. But this was a view I could finally call my own.

It was February 2, a week before Heather's 35th birthday, when she was looking despairingly onto all of this from our back porch. We had spent the morning arguing. She missed California and resented being back among the Bible-thumpers of Saint Augustine, feeling alone and isolated while I was out on tour. With a penchant for dark makeup and black clothes, she stuck out in town among the pickup trucks, Chick-fil-A restaurants, and lawn signs that read GOD HATES FAGS. Some neighbors believed her to be a Satan worshipper.

I figured this was as good a time as any. "Can we talk?" I asked. She nodded, sensing the weight of the request in my voice. I grabbed her by the hand and led her into our bedroom. We both lay on the bed on our sides, facing each other for a while, saying nothing. "I have to tell you something," I finally said. She looked back into my eyes, waiting and nervous. It was so quiet that I could hear her breathing. I held her tightly against my body until I worked up the courage to let it out.

"I'm a transsexual."

The proclamation hung there for a moment, and then crashed to a surreal adrenaline euphoria. I had sampled every barbiturate and narcotic from A to Z in my lifetime, but this was a high I'd never felt before. With three simple words, the levee had finally broken and everything held behind it could never be contained again. Emotions pouring out, I surrendered to being swept away in the current's flow.

"I thought you were going to tell me you were having an affair," she said with a smile. And in a way, I was. I was sneaking off to seedy hotel rooms to be with another woman. Bras and dresses were scattered on the floor next to my bed on tour. I had been keeping secrets and created a level of dishonesty in my marriage.

Before we could really discuss it further, I heard a voice from the hallway call to me. "Daddy?" Evelyn had woken up from her nap and came charging into the room to break up our conversation.

Later in the day, while Heather and I were making the bed and talking about the chores we needed to get through the next morning, she used a male pronoun in regard to me. "Well that's gonna be weird, huh?" I said. "Not saying 'he' for me anymore."

"What do you mean?" she asked.

"I mean I want to transition. I want to become a woman... fully."

She paused and fell silent. I think the revelation that I was a transsexual truly hit her in this moment. She slowly started to comprehend that this didn't mean I'd simply be cross-dressing around the house. It started to hit me, too. I wanted to transition genders, and there was a lot more to that than just hormones and surgery. Neither of us fully understood what it meant yet, or where to start.

The next day Andrew and James met me at the studio to talk about plans around the album and the future of the band. Jordan came, too, as he was again filling in as our manager. Until then, I'd been telling them that I was writing a concept album about a transsexual prostitute—the metaphor behind the feeling of having whored myself out to a record label was thinly transparent since James, Andrew, and I were all processing our own post-traumatic stress disorder from the past couple years of music industry hell. Previously, I'd been able to sneak a few subtle metaphors about my dysphoria in here and there. But an album focused entirely on it? I didn't know how to explain that, and the new songs were not sticking with the guys.

James could make out a few lyrics to the title track through his in-ear monitors: "You want them to see you like they see every other girl / But they just see a faggot."

"Hey, man," he said between takes. "Are you saying 'faggot' on this song? It sounds like you're saying it a lot. Are people gonna be cool with that?"

I realized that the reason the words weren't connecting with them was that they didn't have the context. So I came out with it. I didn't mean to, I just wanted them to understand. I couldn't hold back the momentum of the day before. Once the truth was spoken, it could be contained no longer.

"It's about me, and how I'm a transsexual. This is something I've been dealing with for a long time," I told them. Once I started explaining it, I couldn't stop. It was like an out-of-body experience where I saw myself, but was powerless to hold back the flood of words. "I want to start living as a woman, and to be referred to as Laura. This is something I've thought about a lot and isn't going away, so I might as well embrace it."

No one knew what to say once I finally stopped rambling. The three of them just sat there in the studio control room, looking down at their feet or at whatever lit-up piece of audio equipment their eyes could find, focusing anywhere but on me. We'd had some heavy conversations over the years—emotional moments where we'd told each other off or outright quit the band—but nothing compared to this. Andrew's usually warm smile was locked in since I started talking, and it looked like it was going to melt off his face. His skin flushed red, trying not to flinch. There was nothing any of them could say. I broke the silence by asking them to come smoke a joint with me. We got high standing in a circle in the open back doorway. "OK, well," I said. "I guess that's all we'll do today. How about we try again tomorrow?"

We shared the most comically awkward group hug, a horrible mess of pats on the back and overly extended stiff arms. They left, and I locked the door behind them. Oh fuck, I thought. I called Heather and told her that I had just come out to them. It felt unreal to speak these secrets aloud, hearing myself verbalize thoughts that had only ever existed in my head.

The guys had an hour and a half back to Gainesville to think about all that had just been unloaded on them. James has since told me that as he sat there stoned on that long drive home, a lot of memories over the past 15 years suddenly started to make sense for him. My lyrics, my behavior on tour; one by one, he had tiny flashes of realization about me in this new light.

Like Heather, the band took in this information without fully understanding its immediate implications. Hell, I was still wrapping my brain around the implications, and was basing my knowledge of what would come next from what I had researched online.

I knew I wanted to start hormone replacement therapy, or HRT, so that my physical changes would match the mental ones. But now I was desperate for it. I also knew that to gain access to these hormones, I needed a letter of approval from a doctor, confirming my mental clarity that I was "true trans." The only other option was buying them on the black market on the internet, which I had also considered. I found a counselor in Gainesville, one of two options that came up when searching for "North Florida gender therapist." The first number I called was a disconnected line. The second was answered by a human voice. I had to come out to the stranger on the other end of the line, explaining on the spot that I was seeking access to hormones. I needed to make sure this was a service they could actually provide, and they could.

After making the appointment, I asked Jordan to connect me with the band's publicists, Ken Weinstein and Tito Belis at Big Hassle Media. The three of us got on a conference call and I dumped everything on them at once—I was a transsexual, I planned on transitioning genders, and I would assume a new name. I would soon be Against Me!'s frontwoman, and needed to figure out a strategy to put this information into the public. I don't know what they expected the call to be about, but it certainly wasn't that. After I finished, I heard nothing on the other end for a few seconds until Ken jumped in. "Um...well. OK, this sounds good, Tom," he said. "I think that...let me...give us a few minutes to think on this and we'll call you back." We hung up, and I can't imagine the conversation the two had after that.

True to his word, Ken came back with an idea. He was friends with a writer at *Rolling Stone* whom he greatly trusted, and suggested a plan for me to come out to the world via a feature in the magazine. It would be tasteful and sensitive, and require several interviews and a photo shoot. I agreed, and he went about making the arrangements.

I liked the *Rolling Stone* plan because it meant talking to one person and would be easier than having a thousand private conversations with everyone I knew. But it created new pressure for me and complicated matters with the counselor. The purpose of my session with him was to prove I was of a reasonable mind to fully grasp the implications of transitioning. But explaining myself in his office during that first meeting, I could hear how questionable my sanity must have sounded.

"Look," I started, "I'm married, I have a two-and-a-half-year-old daughter. I'm a musician, and I play in a band for a living. I'm going to publicly come out as transgender soon in *Rolling Stone* magazine. In May, we're leaving on a month-long tour of the U.S., followed by a month and a half of international touring. If this was the way I felt when I was 8, and the way I felt when I was 13, and the way I felt when I was 15, and the way I felt when I was 20, 25, 28, and still now at 31, then this is going to be the way I'm going to feel forever. I want to transition into living my life as a woman, and I need access to hormone replacement therapy."

The doctor looked at me curiously and wrote something down on his clipboard. I could tell he thought I was crazy. I had read online that doctors are often reluctant to prescribe hormones and might even try to talk me out of it. You had to be direct and insistent from the start that this was what you were sure you wanted; not what you thought you may want. It took a while just to convince him of the reality of the situation—that I had a small level of celebrity fronting a popular band, and that an interview about my dysphoria with the biggest music publication in the world was in the works. "So I need you to write me a prescription for HRT," I repeated firmly, trying to demonstrate that I had done my homework. Of course, it wasn't that simple. I would need to come in for regular appointments.

As I continued to wait for the doctor to declare me sane enough to start HRT, I jumped on the Revival Tour, a traveling folk-punk show led by Hot Water Music frontman Chuck Ragan. The show included a rotating ensemble of musicians playing and collaborating on acoustic sets, all traveling from city to city in the same bus. In addition to Chuck and myself, this iteration also featured Dan Andriano from Alkaline Trio, Cory Branan, and Nathaniel Rateliff.

The Revival Tour has a reputation for being something of a manly event, due in part to its flannel-clad ringleader. Chuck is legendary in the punk scene not only for his time in Hot Water Music, but for his famously thick beard, gravelly voice, and rugged outdoorsmanship. As we traveled the country, Chuck would go fishing during the morning, and after the show he'd scale whatever he caught right there in the bus's sink. Sometimes he would kick off his boots and keep his fish in his bunk with him while he slept. Meanwhile, I'd be two bunks over, reading *The Whipping Girl*, a trans rights manifesto and book of reflections on society's views of trans women by transsexual author Julia Serano. I had never even considered this position: demanding to be respected as a trans person, to have pride in myself, and to stand up and be visible. Self-empowerment through gender identity. This book meant hope for me.

I bonded with Cory Branan on the tour. Also a father, he and I spent our nights talking about the struggles of touring when you've got a kid back home. He mentioned that he had a little girl with a woman he met on the road that he tried to see when he could. We showed each other photos of our daughters. I asked what his girl's name was.

"She's my little Jane," he said in his Mississippi accent.

I liked it. I had told Heather and the band I wanted to be called Laura, after my great-grandmother; the name my mother always told me she would've named me if I were born a girl. I also had the idea to take my mother's maiden name, Grace, in place of Gabel. And now I'd found a middle name: Laura Jane Grace.

When the Revival Tour ended, I did a quick run of solo shows in Europe. This limbo phase before my announcement was a liberating time. I knew that nothing I was saying or doing at the moment mattered in comparison to what the world was about to learn about me. The venues we were playing reached out in advance to ask me to do interviews with local press outlets to promote the shows. I turned them all down, telling them I was only doing one interview at the moment, and that they would see it soon enough.

After two months of meetings with the psychotherapist, he asked me to bring Heather in for private questioning about whether or not she was comfortable with her husband transitioning. She was asked repeatedly, both in our couples sessions and in her one-on-one meetings, and she remained adamant that she was supportive of this change. He also had to meet and observe Evelyn to assure that she was a healthy child, and that she and I had a strong relationship. In my one-on-one sessions with him, he would hold up a full-length mirror without explaining why; just letting me talk into my own reflection. Maybe I was supposed to see a new version of myself emerge from our discussion, or maybe it was just to shame me into changing my mind. I went in for half a dozen visits, each one a thoroughly demoralizing experience, all for something as simple as a signature on a piece of paper from a person declaring that I had the right to change my own body. I wondered if he would do research on me and read my lyrics, finding a long history of arrests, lawsuits, and drug use.

This process would not be instantaneous, he told me, and would take two to three more months of evaluation. In that interim, Josh Eells came to Saint Augustine to interview me for the May 24, 2012, issue of *Rolling Stone*. We first had a chat at my favorite taco truck in town, and then headed out to the studio to continue talking. Josh asked me every question he could think of, starting at the beginning—when I first experienced dysphoria, how it had affected me during adolescence, how it led me to band life.

"Was punk rock used as an armor of sorts?" he asked. Of course it was. I might not have been able to express my gender outwardly in the way I wanted to, but at least spiking out my hair and wearing leather jackets spray-painted with political slogans was some sort of expression. While we talked, I could tell that he was looking for the femininity hidden somewhere in me, perhaps behind my eyes or under my voice.

On the second day, Heather and Josh met for her portion of the interview, during which he asked her questions about things she was still uncertain about—correct pronoun usage, the possibility of surgeries, and the one that would come to plague her in interviews: the implication about her own sexuality.

"I mean, does this mean I'm a lesbian now?" she pondered aloud at one point.

For our next scheduled talk, I told him to meet me at the studio, but this time I planned on surprising him by greeting him in full femme. As I walked through the house to exit through the rear door that evening to meet him, donning a wig, makeup, and breast inserts tucked into the bra underneath my dress, I caught eyes with Evelyn, who was sitting on the couch.

I could see the confusion on her face. Something was different. Her daddy was dressed like a woman, and she was trying to understand why.

If Josh experienced any shock about seeing me in a dress, he didn't let on, but he suddenly had a lot more questions to ask. Echo & the Bunnymen's *Ocean Rain* was playing in the background as the interview progressed, and it must have looped five times as we went back and forth.

Cass Bird was the photographer assigned to take photos of me at home. She has an impressive resume and has made many high-profile celebrities from Salma Hayek to Claire Danes look sexy on the covers of publications like *T: The New York Times Style Magazine*. But I didn't feel very sexy. Cass did a great job and I knew I was in good hands, but overall, the experience was awkward and emasculating, having a photographer trying to capture the femininity in me that I had yet to see. She and her assistant tried shooting in various locations around the house, and then suggested we take photos outside on the marsh. I stepped out of my jeans and long black shirt as she shot me practically naked, rolling around in the sand. The ocean wind blew my chin-length hair back, revealing a receding hairline.

My body was covered in sand by the time we got back in the house, so I jumped in the shower to wash it off. When I emerged from the bathroom, with one towel wrapped around my torso at the chest and another wrapped around my head, Cass stopped me. "That's it," she said. I sat on the couch by the window as she captured me like that, fresh out of the shower.

With every flash of the camera, Heather standing there watching, I felt my male ego being cut down to size bit by bit. "OK, now keep your head straight but look out the window," Cass instructed. While I stared, sensing her lens focusing on my damp body, I thought about all the photo shoots I'd done in my life, and what an arrogant prick I'd been through them. I crossed my smooth-shaven legs on top of each other, and felt the shame. I supposed this was my payback for those times.

A few nights later, I was putting Evelyn to bed. As I pulled the covers over her, she put her hand on my forearm.

"Daddy?" she said.

"Yes, sweetheart?"

"I don't want you to be a girl, OK? I want you to be a boy again."

"Well," I said, fighting against the tears welling up in my eyes, "no matter if I'm a boy or a girl, I will always love you, and I will always be your daddy. Nothing will ever change that."

I waited for her to fall asleep before letting my heart shatter into a million pieces. I sat over her by the glow of her nightlight, crying, and imagining the pain she would experience throughout her life because of my transition. I pictured all the kids who would ridicule her for having a father who picked her up from school in a dress, and how much that would strain her relationship with me. Maybe one day in the future she wouldn't want to call me "Daddy" anymore, and maybe that would even be a positive change for my dysphoria. But goddammit, she would always be my daughter, and I would always be her father. It made me think of my own father, and how I didn't plan on telling him about my transition, but would let him find out by reading the article. I wanted to call him, but lacked the courage.

How do you tell a father that you no longer want to wear the name he passed down to you? How could I explain that as a son, I had always felt so desperate for his love and affection, and how much it would mean to be loved and accepted as his daughter? I knew the adrenaline would cloud my focus and the words would come out wrong.

I went to visit my mother in Naples for a weekend, staying in my teenage bedroom, the room where I'd had so many early experiences of dysphoria. It had long since been redecorated, but

I still felt at home in it. For two days I avoided coming out to her, instead letting it weigh on me the whole trip. I left without saying anything. Once back in Saint Augustine, I called her and came out with it. We talked for almost two hours, mostly in long, quiet stretches where I could hear it settling in with her, and how much of it explained my teenage years.

"What about you and Heather?" she asked.

"We're staying together. We're going to try to make it work."

"And Evelyn?"

"I think it's better to do this now, while she's still young."

"What about the band?"

"I don't know. I want to keep playing music. I think this may even be what we need."

"Are you sure?" she kept asking.

"Yes, Mom."

She told me she loved me and we hung up. She may not have understood everything I'd said, but just like when I was a teenager and she bailed me out of jail, she continued to have my back, always.

I came out to my brother over the phone as well. I just called him up and told him very matter-of-factly that I was a transsexual, giving him the short version of what I'd just told our mother, and that was about it. I did my best to play it down and make it a casual conversation. I'm not sure he fully understood what I was saying.

"I love you no matter what," he finally said. "You'll always be my brother."

I wanted to tell him that he'd have to start thinking of me as his sister, but instead we ended the call. One step at a time.

Whenever I came out to people, there was a feeling that I was asking for their permission, or their forgiveness. This was something that seemed instilled in me from feeling belittled by doctors. I was growing more and more frustrated with the psychotherapist and driving an hour and a half every week between Saint Augustine and Gainesville for our appointments. My gender was constantly on trial. I was being treated like a child, back to being a teenager again, trying to justify myself to an authority figure. He wanted to see "proof." I'd show up for the session and he would ask, "So when are you going to start dressing like a woman?" My heart would sink.

"These are women's jeans, this is a woman's shirt. I can't make my hair grow any faster!" I wanted to shout back, but couldn't because I would blow my chances of getting hormones. It was absurd that he thought that just because I wanted to be a woman, that I no longer wanted to wear black clothing and would adopt perfume and frilly dresses.

Then it finally clicked for me. The therapist just wanted to see me in a wig, mascara, and high heels. He needed to see what *he* thought a woman should look like, and *his* idea of femininity. So at our next meeting, I did just that. I played his game, showing up wearing an A-line dress from the Gap and high heels. He immediately wrote me my letter and referred me to an endocrinologist. Simple as that.

I started undergoing electrolysis sessions, too, getting the hair lasered off my face. The people who performed the removals were used to catering to affluent Republican housewives who wanted their legs and bikini zones clean and tidy for beach visits, and were clearly not used to removing beards for someone transitioning genders.

I didn't even bother telling them my name was Laura. The debit cards I paid with and receipts I signed all still said "Thomas Gabel." I offered no explanation as to why I was using their service, and resigned myself to letting them think whatever they wanted. I'd simply tell them where I wanted to be zapped, and lie back in the chair. After an hour of lasering, my face was left swollen and red. The beard shadow loss was minimal and gradual with each visit.

North Florida's resources for trans people are extremely limited. Like the psychotherapist, there was only one endocrinologist, also in Gainesville, doubling my number of weekly drives.

You go through all these therapy sessions, jumping through hoops to convince a stranger that you're really female, you beg for access to hormones that they dangle over you like a carrot, and then you finally get your letter of approval and show up at the endocrinologist's office. There, you are greeted with: "Fill out these forms, *sir*, and we'll call your name when the doctor is ready to see you."

The endocrinologist experience was even further degrading. Not long ago, I was a rock star on stage in front of thousands of people. Fans screamed my name and waited in line for autographs. I thought of the woman in Seattle who flashed me from the crowd, and what she would think if she saw me sitting alone in a cold, sterile room, begging for hormone treatment.

After numerous visits in which I continually affirmed that I wanted to be a woman, the endocrinologist explained the treatment options. She recommended putting me on a patch, like a nicotine patch but with estrogen. I told her that I sweated like crazy on stage, and there was no way the patches would ever stay on. So instead she agreed to start me on a low dosage of three ingestible hormones—estradiol, spironolactone, and progesterone. They would raise my estrogen levels, lower my testosterone, and support breast tissue growth. I'd take one pill of each every day, and in three months I would come back for blood work to see where my levels were.

I drove away excited, high on adrenaline and fear. I'd finally earned the right. I walked into the local drugstore, heading straight to the pharmacy counter, gave my soon-to-be former name to the pharmacist, and asked for my scripts. He turned around, searched, and found them. While typing the information into his computer, he did a double-take, looking at me, then at the bags in his hand, and holding them behind the counter, out of my reach.

"Now, you realize the side effects of these drugs and that they are usually for women, right?" he asked. "You know that they could potentially..."

"Give me the fucking hormones now, you fucking asshole!" I shouted, and pounded my fist on the counter. Nearby shoppers stopped to look at this hysterical person shaking with anger, tears running down my face. "I've seen all of the fucking doctors that I was supposed to, I passed all the damn tests, here's my fucking driver's license, now can I please have the fucking pills?"

I snatched the bag out of his hands and left the cash on the counter. I walked out, completely dead inside but also so alive.

I waited until the next morning to take my first round of pills. I stood in the kitchen, holding them in my hand, observing them for a while before the big swallow. Two white ones and a blue one. The psychotherapist, the endocrinologist, the asshole pharmacist, myself, too—they'd all placed so much weight on these three little pills, like I was about to do something that could potentially ruin my life; that there was no turning back to who I once was. I gave the pills one final look, and then down the hatch.

I swallowed hard.

EPILOGUE
(or MANDATORY HAPPINESS
with LAURA JANE GRACE)

There's a saying on the road that goes: "If your band can't draw a crowd, draw a dick on the wall." After all these years, I can say without hesitation that I feel thankful to be sitting here among the crudely drawn penises in this dingy backstage dressing room, about to play a sold-out show.

There's a lot of downtime on tour; it's a constant game of hurry up and wait, hurry up and wait. Hurry up and get to the airport, wait in a security line. Hurry up and get to the venue, wait to sound-check. As I flipped through the pages of this journal, I realized just how much of my life had been lost to waiting. Days, maybe even weeks or months in total.

Much of my downtime these days is spent doing interviews, which all go the same way. The journalists are polite, but often misinformed. If they compliment my hair or makeup, I'll cringe, because I know it will soon be followed by a question such as "Did you do it yourself?"

Then they turn their recorder on and ask about how happy

I am now that my transition is "complete." As if the fact that a magazine printed the truth about me allowed me to wake up the next morning, entirely transformed; as if coming out solved everything. But just because I accepted myself as transgender didn't mean I knew how to transition, or where that road would take me.

So I keep my answers simple by saying something positive about how much more liberating it is to be on stage now. That much is true. For an hour per night, while the crowd is shouting my lyrics back at me, I feel confident. When I sing the words to my chorus, "Does God bless your transsexual heart?" and they call back, "True trans soul rebel!," it's empowering. If someone had told me about all this when I was 15, I never would have believed it.

But what I don't talk about are the other 23 hours, when I am still paralyzed with self-doubt. And I don't mention the last two years, and everything my transition cost me.

By coming out, I indirectly triggered changes around me. It wasn't just my body that was in transition, but my life, too. People I'd known for years and saw every day cycled out of my world. It wasn't that they were transphobic or unsupportive, it was just that things were different.

Jay was the first to go, quitting the band very abruptly and unceremoniously, but entirely appropriately for him. It was more a relief than anything, but it left us without a drummer two weeks before a scheduled Australian festival.

After Jay, it was Andrew. Neither of us was sure we wanted to be in a band together anymore, both chasing separate visions. Andrew was fed up with everything I'd put him through over the years and resented the control I asserted over the band. It all blew up in my face in the airport coming home from tour when he laid into me for what felt like the last time. It was another argument over the direction of the band, but really an argument about nothing at all; just the two of us in a pissing match over who was more frustrated about the rut we were still in. We had traveled so far and fought so hard, and all for what? A band that was still struggling to scrape by.

We boarded our flight home with feelings unresolved, and I didn't hear from him for weeks after that. Eventually he called to tell me he was done with Against Me!. We had been through a lot of hell together over the years—breakups, arrests, fistfights, overturned buses, lawsuits, deaths. Publicly coming out and announcing my transition was part of my healing process. I think that for Andrew, quitting the band was the transition he needed. I respect that. I'm sure he recognized that while we could make it through one particular trial, there would always be another waiting not too far down the road. That's the way it always went for Against Me!. One step forward, two steps back. A pat on the back followed by a swift punch in the gut.

When Andrew left, a sad realization hit me: just how much I was going to miss him. Even though he had been a constant in my life for 10 years, he was a stranger before joining the band. Once our working relationship was over, I knew I wouldn't see much more of him. Andrew chose happiness—his wife and daughter—instead of the endless struggles of the band, and I can't say I blamed him. I thought about throwing in the towel with him, but I was contractually obligated to hand in one last record.

Jordan was burned out, run into the ground. Always the unspoken fifth member of the band, he had gone from putting out our first records, to being our merch guy, to tour managing, to finally being our manager. It was all just too much. He told me he was quitting over the phone, and I didn't need an explanation. I understood. He stepped back from any relationship, business or friendship, got married, bought a house, and started a new life. He's still putting out records through Sabot and picking up occasional tour managing gigs for other bands.

This is life on the road. For years, your entire existence is intertwined with someone else's, to the point where you can't commit to anything without consulting their schedule, and the next day you wake up and never talk again. This was how it had been since I was kid, when the people I loved just one day just disappeared. I started wondering if I was driving them all away.

Even my studio seemed to give up on me. After a weekend of heavy Florida storms, I drove out to the studio to find that a huge tree had blown over and crashed through the roof of the building. The place was a mess of branches and pools of water. The floor where I once stood and came out to the band had buckled and warped under the dampness. All the repairs my father and brother spent hours making while rebuilding our relationship were destroyed. As I surveyed the ruins of the room, it felt like the universe was trying to send me a message; like God himself had sent the floods to wash the band from the earth. I hadn't had a drink in over a year and a half, but Heather and James told me they liked me better drunk, that I needed to loosen my grip and relax. This seemed like as good a time as any to take a stiff shot of whiskey. And just like that, I was back to drinking.

I wrote my father after the *Rolling Stone* article ran, telling him that while as part of my transition I would be shedding the name he had given me, there were so many other things I had to be thankful for; specifically, the life of travel that his job opened me to. For all its instability, I always appreciated my upbringing. I ended by sharing a memory that had come to mind recently about the last months we spent in Italy, and asked a question that I had always wondered about: What was it that he spent late nights writing about in his office all those years ago? The only response I got back was:

Your presentation left much to be desired. For now the door is open but we'll see.

—Dad

I reread his message over and over, trying to decipher what it meant. Even looking at it now, I'm still not sure. It made me angry to feel like I even had to ask for acceptance and understanding when a father's love is supposed to be unconditional. I wrote out 30 frustrated replies, but couldn't bring myself to send any. We haven't spoken since.

And then there was Heather. Publicly, I did my best to pretend life was still good between us. Only two weeks after I started HRT, Against Me! left for a month-long U.S. tour to support the Cult. Heather came along to sell our merch and brought Evelyn. This was my dream—the three of us touring as a family.

Realistically, I should have taken a break from the road to give myself and my family time to adjust to these changes. I certainly wasn't ready. I wanted more time to grow my hair longer and get a few more laser sessions in, so that I could feel more comfortable in my femininity. But I felt a responsibility to the rest of the band. We had worked so hard to get back on our feet, and if I slowed up now, even briefly, it would have killed our momentum.

Fortunately, punks don't care about the Cult. Since the tickets were out of our fans' price range, I largely got to fly under the radar the whole time. Joan Jett came out to one of the shows in New York, and sang a cover of the Replacements' "Androgynous" with me. After the show, we stayed up smoking weed and talking. Joan could tell that despite whatever positive face I was putting on for fans, I was stressed and needed a friend.

"Gender is a spectrum," she told me. "Don't worry about

trying to fit into someone else's box they made for you." Just hearing her say those words was assuring. We even made plans to write a song together, which would end up on her next album.

When we got back on the bus, Evelyn, who was supposed to be asleep, popped her head out from her bunk curtain to greet us.

"Hi, Joan Jett!"

"Hi, little Evelyn."

I watched Joan tuck my daughter back into bed and hoped that one day Evelyn would remember this moment of a stoned Joan Jett putting her to sleep and asking, "Are you going to dream of doggies and kitties?"

Heather led the charge in the day-to-day details of my transition on tour, making sure the bands and crew addressed me by female pronouns and correcting them when they didn't. Whenever a situation arose that posed an uncertainty in etiquette or procedure, everyone looked to her and followed suit.

It felt supportive, though sometimes the support was misplaced and became overbearing. It was infantilizing at times, having my wife coddle me through this readjustment. But I had told Heather that I was transitioning, and now she was holding me to it, making sure I followed through, almost annoyed sometimes when I wasn't moving fast enough. The idea that I was supposed to be moving along at any pace only made my anxiety grow.

My transition put Heather in a difficult position. The media, in their articles about me, always portrayed her as the supportive wife, standing by her spouse, unflinching in the face of this major life change, but of course it wasn't that simple for her. She wasn't given a chance to fully process the changes and how she felt in relation to them. I almost took for granted that she had to make the same phone calls I had made, informing her parents and siblings that her husband would be living as a woman. Friends and family raised questions about her own sexuality. Was she now a lesbian? Would she still call me her husband? She didn't yet know the answers, and she didn't ask to be in this situation.

The normal marital quibbles we'd always had over trivial things like me buying the wrong kind of almond milk or her leaving behind garbage in the car intensified. There was a deeper frustration growing underneath everything, manifesting itself in this daily bickering.

Heather and I had always been able to mend our fights with makeup sex, but the deeper I got into my hormone treatment, the more difficult that became. The hormones had depleted my sex drive, and even when sexual desire hit me, my erections were less firm. I couldn't tell if it was from a lack of testosterone or a lack of confidence. I internalized it all as shame. Our intimacy quickly lost the passion we once had between us. The times when we did have sex felt forced; like we were going through the motions.

In the mornings, before I headed to the studio to work on the new album, we would drop Evelyn off at school and then come back home and get stoned in our bathroom near the air vent, pulling rips out of her Grim Reaper bong. We lit each bowl up with the leftover personalized matches from our wedding, striking them against the cardstock with our initials embossed on it. One by one, I watched the box of matchsticks dwindle down. It felt like our marriage was burning up with them, like we were smoking it down to the last match.

I felt us growing apart. It was the same feeling I had in my early 20s, when my first marriage was failing. It was the same coldness that echoed through my parents' house in Italy during the disintegration of their marriage. Heather started taking week-long trips to Chicago, where she had family, and wanted to spend time with a new group of friends she made. She was excited about collaborating on art projects with some guy she met

there, planning future showings of their work in town. Under our
bed, I found a box of mixtapes and letters from him, addressed
to Heather in her maiden name. I wasn't certain she was having
an affair, but this emotional connection was replacing ours. I
realized she was building a new life, a support structure to fall
back on. I didn't tell her what I'd found, but I gave her an out.
I told her that if she wanted to get her own place in Chicago,
I'd understand.

I declined most interviews in the year following the *Rolling
Stone* article, except for an appearance on MTV's revived *House
of Style*, where I showed off my new wardrobe. I also agreed to
write an article for *Cosmopolitan* meant to catch the world up
on the progress of my transition a year after coming out and its
effect on my marriage. We were still trying to maintain a public
image of the happy couple.

In the article, I referred to Heather as my soul mate while
ignoring the problems at home and trying to put an optimistic
spin on our collapsing sex life. I showed her what I'd written
before it was published, hoping my expression of eternal commitment would keep the last embers in the fire between us burning.
She didn't have much of a reaction, though, and just sort of
shrugged it off.

Heather suggested that we seek marriage counseling. I scoffed
at the idea that any therapists in Florida would be able to handle
the unique nuances of our marriage. Plus, I had no time. The
due date for *Transgender Dysphoria Blues* was rapidly approach-
ing, and there was still work to be done.

With no band left to speak of after the departures of Andrew,
Jay, and Jordan, I finished work on the album with James, who
stuck with me until the bitter end. The last dollars of our budget
were spent booking time at a studio in Valdosta, Georgia, that
we chose because it was reputable but cheap. The place was a

converted auto garage where the walls and ceiling were painted black, and the carpets covered huge oil stains on the concrete floor. From my days spent repairing engines, I recognized the lingering smell of fumes and rusty metal. Our engineer and the studio owner was a man named Lee, who had a shaved head and a .45 holstered on his hip at all times. It felt like the end of the line for Against Me!. This bleak, dark room was the place we would be shot and left for dead.

I had faith in the songs, though. They were more personal and honest than anything I'd ever written. No longer confined by the burden of having to mince words and mask emotions behind metaphor, I was free to be as direct and aggressive as I wanted. In a way, it was the record I'd been working on my whole life—lyrics about fear and frustration, confusion and identity. There was no filter, and I fired away with everything I'd been holding in for three decades. I traded everything I had for these 10 songs. They were all I had to show for a dwindling career, a failing marriage, and a decaying life.

I wrote an existential love song for Evelyn called "Two Coffins," and one for Pope called "Dead Friend." I felt Pope's ghost watching everything falling apart for me, still trying to keep my spirits up, so when I needed a title for the song I wrote about Heather, it seemed obvious to call it "Fuckmylife666." I imagined Pope calling back, "Mandatory happiness!"

James and I stayed in a nearby $50-a-night Days Inn right off the exit from I-75. Heather tried calling me, but blind drunk, I deliberately didn't pick up. I woke up at 4 AM. My T-shirt was completely soaked, and my arms were stiff and trembling. I took a cold shower and came out of the bathroom to realize that the thermostat was set to 68 degrees. My body was reacting violently to the mixture of alcohol, anxiety, and hormones. I didn't sleep that night and was a wreck in the morning. I got through the day in the studio by letting James finish up his guitar parts while I rested on the couch. For the first time in over a year, I didn't take my hormones.

I skipped them the next morning, too, after another sleepless night, and was feeling even worse. I couldn't hold my hands steady to finish a guitar take. My fingers wouldn't clench a chord or strum properly. My voice was shot, and I was convinced a polyp had developed on my vocal cords. The only way I got through the day was on a couple of Valium. Even with them, I was manic; I felt possessed. Over and over I failed to play the intro riff for "Fuckmylife666." After I was finally able to perform it to Lee's satisfaction, I put my guitar down, walked to the van parked in front of the studio, and broke down.

I don't cry often, but at that moment, I was an uncontrollable, sobbing mess. I couldn't think straight. My only clear thought was how badly I'd fucked up my life. I wasn't even able to recall a time before my transition. Memories of time spent locked behind bathroom doors in dresses, or sneaking down hotel hallways in heels, were fading from my mind. I couldn't remember why I'd wanted so badly to put myself through this. I didn't want to go through with it anymore; I just wanted my family. I wanted to be the person Heather fell in love with. I hoped that maybe there was still a chance to take back everything I had said and done, and go back to being her husband and Evelyn's daddy. I had let my dedication to the fantasy override my responsibilities. I thought back to that night when I was 13 and made a deal with the devil. Twenty years later, he had come to collect his due.

I called my mother.

"Mom, can you do something for me?" I asked, though I was slurring so much, I wasn't sure she could understand me.

"Of course," she said in the calm, motherly voice I needed to hear. "What is it?"

"Can you pray for me? Pray for my soul. Pray, because I don't know what else to do." I couldn't even process what she said in response.

When we hung up, I had a flash of realization: I had been heading for this crash the whole time, but no one had warned me. I was convinced that it was a conspiracy, that my doctors had all seen this coming and set me up to fail. I called my psychotherapist in Gainesville, sure that when he had written his letter of approval, he was secretly laughing about the nervous breakdown I was in for at the one-year mark, once my male ego completely shattered.

"You can probably set your fucking watch to this, can't you?" I cried at him. "You know exactly how many months it takes for someone on hormones to have their mental fucking breakdown, don't you? This is a great moment of satisfaction for you, isn't it?"

I called my endocrinologist's office next, demanding to speak to the doctor, but was told she wasn't available. I tried to schedule an appointment, but the soonest the receptionist said she could book me was in three months.

James drove me to an emergency care clinic where a doctor, who at first presumed me to be a junkie looking for a fix, wrote me a prescription for Ambien. Even with the sleep aid, I couldn't sleep at night. I kept getting worse and worse, a rapid unraveling in the last days in Valdosta. As my health worsened and I lost the motivation to soldier on, I doubted the songs on this album would ever be performed publicly. I started to think of the album as my suicide note that would be left behind for the world to find—the last will and testament of Laura Jane Grace.

I made the decision to quit hormones cold turkey. Cutting yourself off from hormones after your body has built up a dependency to them fucks you up in ways you can't prepare for. Without a constant flow of estrogen coming in and androgen being blocked, the testosterone came raging back into my system, making me feel like I was going through puberty all over again. The man in me wasn't ready to die, not without a fight. My face broke out with acne and my skin became oily; I noticed that my body's odor changed; I gained weight. Between flashes of depression and a rebounded, out-of-control sex drive, my mood fluctuated suddenly and wildly between sadness and anger. My body could no longer naturally produce dopamine, and the chemical imbalance left me physically incapable of feeling happy.

After two weeks of powering through, clinging to my sanity by a thread, the album was done. The minute I finished recording the last note, it was out of my hands. For all I knew, it was the last I'd ever hear it.

I headed home to Saint Augustine, and walked into an empty house. Heather was still in Chicago with Evelyn. I sat on the bed where I had once worn Heather's dress while fantasizing about life as a woman, but now I had a new fantasy in mind. I thought about driving to a nearby motel where I'd draw a warm bath and down a cocktail of Ambien, Xanax, and wine. I could take a razor blade to my wrists and be gone before they returned home. I thought about the blood that would fill the cracks between the tiles of the bathroom floor. All anyone would find would be my cold, lifeless body and a note on the nightstand. They would be better off without me.

In the 24 hours I had to myself at home, I picked up smoking cigarettes again. Maybe it was to cope with the stress, or maybe it reminded me of the last time I'd smoked—our honeymoon in Rome. I sat on the back porch, chain-smoking, and listening for Heather's car to pull into the driveway so I could kiss her and try to feel that it wasn't really over between us.

"Take a shower. You smell like cigarettes," she told me when she came back.

Heather was at her breaking point. Not only was she still

suffocated by Florida living, but she was now what the neighbors referred to as the wife of "that tranny." As we sat on our back porch watching the sun go down, I asked what I could do to make her happy again.

"I cannot spend another fucking day here," she said, before dropping the ultimatum. "If you want to save our marriage, we have to move to Chicago tomorrow."

It was an optimistic lie. There was nothing left to save. Chicago was where her priorities had shifted. She had a new life waiting for her there—friends, family, a love interest. Left without much choice, I agreed to get a place there sight unseen. We had a yard sale in Florida to prepare for the move, selling our belongings for pennies on the dollar or just giving them away. Paintings, records, wedding gifts, all the possessions that comprised our life together, sold off or discarded. Years of screen-printed Against Me! tour posters, T-shirts, and stacks of magazines with articles about us went, too; the band's history left at the curb with the trash. Two hundred and sixty dollars was the total value of our shared existence. She hired a moving company to transport what was left, though something about the movers seemed sketchy—maybe it was that their logo was stuck on the side of their truck with masking tape. Much of my equipment and guitars never made it to Chicago, having been "lost along the way."

We drove separate cars out of Florida, with Evelyn riding with Heather, and me alone. I arrived first to find an old house that was falling apart. There were broken windows, stained carpets, questionable electrical outlets. It was just like the 911 House, but lonely without the other punks. I waited for Heather but she didn't show up. When I called her to ask where she was, she told me she had gone straight to her guy friend's house.

Heather fell out of love with me over that summer. It wasn't her fault. I had taken her for granted. It was always about me—my career, my band, my transition. The effort I was putting in now by moving to Chicago was too little, too late. I realized that the marriage was unsalvageable, but couldn't accept it. I spent my nights wallowing on our couch, plucking at my guitar, while Heather stayed out later and later, partying with her new friends, coming home wasted as the sun was rising, or just not coming home at all.

"I am attracted to men, not women." Heather said she had realized this. She told me I'd lost my swagger, and that I was a shell of the person I used to be. I was no longer the cocky, loudmouth punk she met on that Alkaline Trio tour. I looked in the mirror hoping to see the woman she claimed to see staring back, but only saw the disgusting tranny I'd always seen before. How could anyone love someone so full of self-hate? How could anyone else see me as a woman if I couldn't see myself as one?

The East Coast solo tour I had booked before my breakdown was the last thing I wanted to do that August. For most in attendance, it was the first time seeing me since my coming out. It was nerve-wracking to stand on stage alone, with nothing but a microphone and an acoustic guitar, all eyes on me. Without the volume of a band behind me, I could distinctly hear people in the crowd shouting words of support. But every compliment I heard—"You look beautiful!" or "I love you!"—just made me feel like more of a fraud. After a show at the Bowery Ballroom in New York, a fan found me outside smoking a cigarette. They told me that I was their hero, and that I gave them the courage to come out and start HRT. But I didn't feel like anyone's hero. I still wasn't taking the hormones. I wanted to scream some sense into them and beg them not to do it. "Look at me! Hormones ruined my fucking life and will ruin yours, too! Are you really willing to risk everything and everyone you love for this?" But instead, I just smiled and posed for a picture.

I was a wreck through the whole week. After blurring my way through each show, I went back to my room and weighed the positives and negatives of stopping my transition, stuck in limbo between wanting to continue as a woman and wanting to go back to being a man. Backing away from my transition meant career death; that I knew. I'd already made this grand announcement that evoked my fans' support. I couldn't just ask them all to forget about it. The trans community would full-on excommunicate me as well. I'd seen it happen to other trans people who decided to de-transition. It was a crime akin to a punk band selling out to a major label. I fantasized about running away and starting a new life somewhere. I could shave my head and have surgery to remove my breasts, get a job as an auto mechanic, and no one would even know who I was. That wouldn't be so bad, I thought. When this indecision kept me awake, I took as many Ambien as I could, washing them down with a bottle of vodka. But try as I might, I kept waking up.

When the tour ended, I returned home to Chicago, where I was a stranger in a strange city. Establishing yourself in a new area when you're transitioning is difficult. Although I wasn't taking HRT at the moment, I needed to find a new psychotherapist, a new endocrinologist, a new laser hair removal place, a new everything.

Eventually I found a therapist specializing in gender who was more helpful than anyone I'd talked to in Florida. She told me that it was good that I'd hit rock bottom, that I'd walked right up to the edge and turned back around. It was okay to have thoughts of suicide, she said, as long as it gave me the proper perspective—that while I was living in the present, I should be living to the fullest. She tried to prescribe heavy antidepressants, but I refused to subject my body to more chemicals.

I wish I could say that Heather and I ultimately turned things around, that we fell back in love and started fresh in Chicago.

But with transitioning, nothing is guaranteed. On November 8—my birthday—we both conceded that it was better for us to live apart. We sat Evelyn down and told her that we were going to try being a family in a new way. Heather did all the talking; I was so heartbroken that I could barely speak or look at her while she explained it. Evelyn protested, but we assured her that we both still loved her, and always would. I got an apartment nearby, and Heather and I agreed that Evelyn would split her time between us.

I knew from experience what the sting of a divorce felt like, but this was different. When a relationship ends, both people go back to their own lives, the ones they lived before they fell in love. Heather could return to being herself again, but who would I be?

Once it was over between us, my therapist encouraged me to get back on hormones, promising—guaranteeing, even—that one day I would look in the mirror and find the woman I had always wanted to see. She suggested that I start taking hormones in the form of injectables. On December 13, I shot them up for the first time, and the process was terrifying. In a way, though, it made the commitment to hormones feel more real than it ever had, like I was going on HRT for the first time. The responsibility of properly shooting a two-inch-long needle into my own thigh muscle carried a lot more weight than just popping three little pills.

Starting back on hormones immediately ushered in a change within me. My mood picked up, my thought process became more clear, I was able to process emotions more reasonably. It felt right; like I'd gained something that had been missing my whole life.

For Christmas, I got Heather one final gift and told her not to open it around her parents. It was a human skull I'd bought from an antique dealer. I could think of no gift with more finality. I hoped whenever she saw it, it would remind her of the eternal love I felt for her, that underneath gender constructs—the skin and thread, stitches and ligaments—we are all just bones in a box. She loved it.

By the end of 2013, I'd fully built the band back up, recruiting Atom Willard to drum for us. Atom had saved us at the last minute earlier in the year, filling in on our Australia tour after Jay quit. Atom is a professional, one of the drummers you call when you need someone who can learn a 25-song set in a week. He heard we needed the help and volunteered to come along. Given that we were working with a fill-in player, we went into the tour hoping we could just get through the shows without any colossal failures, but the shows went better than expected. They went so well, in fact, that I asked him to record drum tracks that we'd use on *Transgender Dysphoria Blues*. Atom fit in so smoothly during our recording sessions and live shows that I offered him the spot full-time, and he accepted.

Inge Johansson replaced Andrew the same way Andrew had replaced Dustin—he just reached out and asked if we needed a new bassist at the right time. Inge is a Swedish vegan who played in the band the (International) Noise Conspiracy, a group whose music and politics I had long admired. Not only was he a good fit for Against Me! musically, but the more he and I talked, the more we connected over our similar anarchist philosophies. He was genuinely invested in his ideals. This was an element that had been lost in the band over the years, and something I welcomed back.

On the last day of the year, as the snow fell hard in Chicago, Inge, Atom, James, and I packed our equipment onto our bus for our first month-long tour together. As the guitars and amps were loaded on, I felt a sense of security. After months of drifting through this unfamiliar new city where I'd lost sight of my own identity, I was glad to be back on the road with my band where I knew how to exist, where I understood who I was. As the bus pulled out, leaving behind a snow-covered Chicago, I crawled into my bunk that would be my home for the next four weeks, stared at the ceiling in front of me, and exhaled in relief.

One of the first things I noticed at our shows was that our audience was different. Our crowd was the most diverse it had ever been. There were punks from our No Idea Records days, metalheads who saw me at my drunkest on the Mastodon tour, kids who stood in line for autographs in the heat of Warped Tour, and Foo Fighters fans who gave that opening band dressed in black a chance. Even the angry punks who still popped up every album cycle to call me a sellout gave me a pass this time around. Maybe they understood me now, and forgave my past career choices in this new context, or maybe I'd just finally worn them down. It felt like the band was starting with a clean slate. Against Me! could be anything I wanted it to be now.

There was also a new community of trans and gender-queer fans that I'd picked up in the year and a half since I came out. Some of them weren't even interested in punk; they just came out to support me. I appreciated their presence and tried to make myself as accessible as possible, sticking around after the shows to talk to these people and learn from them. Many told me that my visibility helped them understand their own gender identity, and meeting them often did the same for me. I even lost the urge to scare them away from starting hormones.

With Inge and Atom joining me and James, Against Me! rebalanced itself. Touring felt like it was supposed to. Even though the roads and venues were familiar, everything felt new again. The predictability of touring that had worn me down over the years was gone. I was pushed outside my comfort zone, open to new adventures and new romances—meeting people, gaining fans, and bonding with my bandmates. It felt the same way it did back when I loaded up the Buick LeSabre, and it reminded me of why I started touring in the first place.

Transgender Dysphoria Blues hit stores while we were three weeks into the tour, the first album of our last three not to leak online prior to its release date. The critical response was immediate and positive. It hit number 23 on the *Billboard* chart, our highest-ranking album ever. Mainstream press outlets—even ones I was sure had given up on us—almost unanimously heaped praise on it and commended me for my songwriting. Though it was all very humbling, and I was grateful for the support, I took it with a grain of salt. It took six albums, but I was finally smart enough to recognize that while acclaim is nice, it's also fleeting. One album, you're a critical darling, and the next they say you're washed up, so it's best not to get too comfortable with the flattery.

At the end of tour, we returned to *The Late Show with David Letterman* for my first televised performance as a woman. I was nervous about being in the spotlight—doing press and photo shoots. I'd only been back on hormones for a month, and was still figuring out how to exist as a trans person, let alone a public figure. But oddly, being in front of the cameras felt soothing in its familiarity. I wasn't fazed or awestruck to be on TV anymore. *I'm a musician, this is what I do,* I thought. I was more concerned about what shoes to wear or how to do my makeup than I was about performing. I settled on a simple black T-shirt and a black pair of jeans instead of a dress. It was more important to feel the internal changes than to exhibit them outwardly. We played "Fuckmylife666," and my fingers were far more steady on guitar than they were when the song was recorded in Georgia.

We clocked in over 150 shows across 57,000 miles that year—the United States, Mexico, Canada, Australia, Europe, and Japan—three full laps around the world. *We're never going home,* I thought to myself once again. For more than half my life, Against Me! had been the thing that pushed me forward, the thing that held me back, and the thing that almost killed me. But this time, it was the thing that saved me.

I'm at the final page of this journal. When I get home, I'll toss it atop the pile with the rest. Dozens of books, filled top to bottom in ink, teeming with my every thought, fear, and emotion of the last three decades. I've decided to burn them all, a funeral pyre for Thomas James Gabel. A true prick. I hope we never meet again.

There's a sticker on the cover of this one, a purple heart placed there with care by Evelyn. She told me I would see it while away on tour and think of her. And on another night, I will, but tonight she is right here with me for this show. I'm watching her on the couch across from me as she climbs on James, my loyal guitarist, my faithful friend, the punk with the green mohawk who went running down our high school halls.

It means so much to me for Evelyn to stand on the side of the stage and watch us play. I want her to keep those memories of people cheering for me and singing my songs. I only hope one day when she faces ridicule, when she has to justify her father to her peers, that she will recall these moments and it will go down easier.

Evelyn grabs something from the coffee table and comes running over to me with it. It's the new issue of *Rolling Stone*. On the cover is a close-up shot of Madonna. She looks exactly the way I remember when I first saw her at five years old, the same age Evelyn is now. Red lipstick, piercing blue eyes, not a single blond hair out of place. Her skin is delicate and gorgeous.

"Daddy, who is this?" she asks me.

"That's Madonna, Evelyn," I tell her. "She's a musician."

"Just like you?"

"Just like me."

It's time to take the stage. The band huddles in a circle, and we throw our hands into a pile. Evelyn squeezes in and puts hers on top.

"To rock and roll," I say, and we break into a cheer.

James heads out of the room with Inge and Atom filing closely behind. I take one last look in the mirror, a little less afraid of the person I see staring back.

"You ready, Evelyn?" I ask. She looks up at me and nods.

Then we walk down the hallway together holding hands—me and her.

ACKNOWLEDGMENTS

LAURA JANE GRACE:

Thank you Cait Hoyt for always believing in my ability to actually pull it together and finish writing a book, and for finding the best home for said book.

Thank you Dan Ozzi for reading through decades' worth of my journals, helping me to make sense of it all and shape it into a story, and for still talking to me afterwards.

Thank you Mike Ferraro for the early editing help when first starting work on this book.

Thank you Chris Norris for all the years of graphic design conspiracy.

Thank you Mauro DiPreta and Hachette for giving me the creative freedom to write the story I wanted to write and being infinitely patient and understanding through the finishing of it.

Thank you to all the artists and bands that I've had the honor of sharing the stage and touring with over the years. Also, to the crew working behind the scenes who helped make each show possible and for teaching me that there is no person more important than another on the road.

I can't possibly thank every single person individually named in this book, but I owe all of you a great deal of gratitude for the impact you've made on my life, the good and the bad. I'm thankful for what I've learned from each one of you. It has shaped the person I am today. If I had to live it all over again, I wouldn't change anything for the world.

DAN OZZI:

Thank you first and foremost to the inimitable Laura Jane Grace for inviting me to work on this book with her despite there being literally hundreds of other candidates more skilled and qualified. I can say with no degree of uncertainty that working with her changed my life. For the better, mostly.

Thank you to Chris Norris for whatever it is he did on this book.

Thank you to Mauro DiPreta and everyone at Hachette for going along with our ideas that were at times so esoteric and unmarketable that most other publishers would have balked.

Thank you to all of my friends and family, who are so great in number and their support so overwhelming in magnitude that I wouldn't possibly know how to go about properly expressing the extent of my gratitude to them.

Thank you to Annie Flook for her saintly patience while I put our lives on hold to get this book done.

And thank you to my best friend, Tami Lynn Andrew, who introduced me to Laura's music when we were just kids by reading me her lyrics over the phone, and whose name now adorns her book forever and ever.

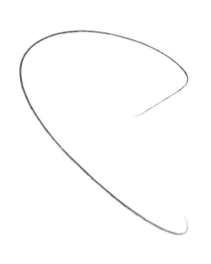